Jesus and Caesar Augustus

VINCENT A. YZERMANS

Jesus and Caesar Augustus

A Legend

TWENTY-THIRD PUBLICATIONS
Mystic, Connecticut

Excerpt from *The Jerusalem Bible*, © 1966 by Darton, Longman & Todd, Ltd. and Doubleday, a division of Bantam, Doubleday, Dell Publishing Group, Inc. Reprinted by permission.

Twenty-Third Publications
P.O. Box 180
185 Willow St.
Mystic, CT 06355
(203) 536-2611

©1989 by Vincent A. Yzermans. All rights reserved. No part of this publication may be reproduced in any manner without prior written permission of the publisher. Write to Permissions Editor.

ISBN 0-89622-396-5
Library of Congress Catalog Card No. 89-50566

TO

ROBERT J. VOIGT

Priest — Brother — Friend

Contents

Chapter 1
The Home at Nazareth — 1

Chapter 2
The Terrible Palace of Herod — 23

Chapter 3
The Meeting of Two Worlds — 35

Chapter 4
The Beautiful Blue Sea — 63

Chapter 5
The Appian Way — 79

Chapter 6
The Inn of the Three Taverns — 103

Chapter 7
The Center of the World — 125

Chapter 8
The Palace of the Emperor — 145

Chapter 9
The Return Voyage — 161

Cast of Characters

This is a legend woven from the threads of stories the writer heard from his youngest days. We know nothing about the hidden life of Christ, that span of eighteen years from the finding in the temple until the opening of his public life, which was about his thirtieth year. But...

A story such as this most probably did not happen, except in the writer's mind. What actually did occur during those eighteen years we will only know when Jesus is fully revealed to us in the kingdom to come.

For the most part, the names of the characters who appear in this legend are the names of real persons who are mentioned in the pages of the New Testament.

JESUS OF NAZARETH—The Anointed One and Prince of Peace.

MARY OF NAZARETH—The virgin mother of Jesus.

JOSEPH OF NAZARETH—The foster father of Jesus who ancient traditions say was a carpenter.

SIMON AND JUDE—The sons of Cleophas and first cousins of Jesus. Numbered among the apostles of Jesus, they are referred to as the "brethren" of Jesus in Matthew 13:55.

JOSEPH OF ARIMATHEA—He is called a rich man and disciple of Jesus in Matthew 27:57. He helped bury Jesus' body in the new tomb he prepared for himself. Arimathea is a small town not far from Jerusalem.

PHILIP, THE HARBOR MASTER—Philip is referred to as one of the seven deacons chosen by the apostles. In Chapter 8 of the Acts of the Apostles his conversion of the Ethiopian officer is told and in Chapter 21 Saint Paul and his companions stayed in his house.

NICODEMUS, THE STEWARD—Nicodemus appears three times in the gospel of Saint John. In Chapter 3 he converses with Jesus about being born again; in Chapter 7 he disputes with the Pharisees about the origins of Jesus; in Chapter 19 he assists Joseph of Arimathea in preparing the body of Jesus for burial.

ALEXANDER, THE CAPTAIN—He bears the name of no scriptural person. The son I have given him, Aquilla, is frequently referred to in the writings of Paul as being associated with Paul in Corinth, Ephesus, and Rome.

ARISTARCHUS, THE FIRST MATE—Aristarchus is frequently mentioned in the Acts of the Apostles as a fellow traveler of Paul in Ephesus; as his companion in Greece; finally, as his fellow prisoner in Rome. The sacred writer noted that he was a Thessalonian.

SIMON THE COOK—Three evangelists, Matthew, Mark, and Luke, refer to Simon of Cyrene as a man who helped Jesus carry the cross.

BARNABAS, THE AGENT—The Acts of the Apostles tell us that Barnabas was an elder in the church at Antioch, a companion of Paul, and the latter's defender in time of great need. Tradition tells us that Barnabas ultimately became the bishop, or overseer, of the church on the island of Cyprus.

RUFUS AND ALEXANDER—A passing remark in the gospel of Mark tells us that Rufus and Alexander were the sons of Simon of Cyrene. Since the Gospel of Mark was most probably written for a Roman audience, his readers probably knew Rufus and Alexander.

GAIUS OCTAVIUS CAESAR AUGUSTUS—The report that Urban drew up for Joseph, which Jesus read along the Appian Way, is essentially a biographical and historical appraisal of Augustus. The emperor was born 23 September 63 B.C., and died 19 August 14 A.D., in the arms of his wife, Livia, after governing the empire 57 years.

SILVANUS, THE INNKEEPER—His name does not appear in the Scriptures. His warmth, friendliness, and gracious hospitality I have modeled after a modern Roman innkeeper, Dominic DiLuca of the Hotel Sitea.

URBAN, MARY, JULIA—I have taken these names from the list of those Saint Paul greets in Chapter 16 of his letter to the Romans.

LONGINUS—Augustus created the Praetorian Guard in 6 B.C. to be the elite among the Roman army. Its members, consisting of nine cohorts, served as his personal bodyguards. I have placed Longinus as a captain of that corps. Tradition ascribes the same name to the soldier who pierced the side of Jesus with a lance on Calvary. Traditions also tell us that after the resurrection Longinus became a follower of Jesus and lived as a hermit near Caesarea for 28 years.

The route of the *Jubilee* is intentionally the same course that the ship bearing Saint Paul to Rome followed some fifty years later.

Acknowledgments

I wish to express my appreciation to the following people who have assisted in the publication of this book:

For financial grants in aid: Rear Admiral (ret.) Emory Stanley of Seattle, Washington; Mr. and Mrs. Thomas Carey of Anchorage, Alaska; Mr. and Mrs. Loren Bergmann of Melrose, Minnesota.

For reading the manuscript and making many valuable suggestions: Rev. Wilfred A. Illies; Rev. Robert J. Voigt; Mrs. Frank Fehrman; Mr. Robert Spaeth; Mr. Jon Hassler; Mr. James P. Shannon.

For the illustrations that appear in this book: Mrs. Vonett Yell and Mr. Melvin Bergmann.

For encouragement and support during the many revisions of the manuscript: Rev. Michael Marx, O.S.B.

ITALY
ROME
PUTEOLI
MACEDONIA
GREECE
MESSINA
STRAIT
SICILIA I.
SYRACUSE
ATHENS
CORINTH
ACHAIA
MEDITERRAN

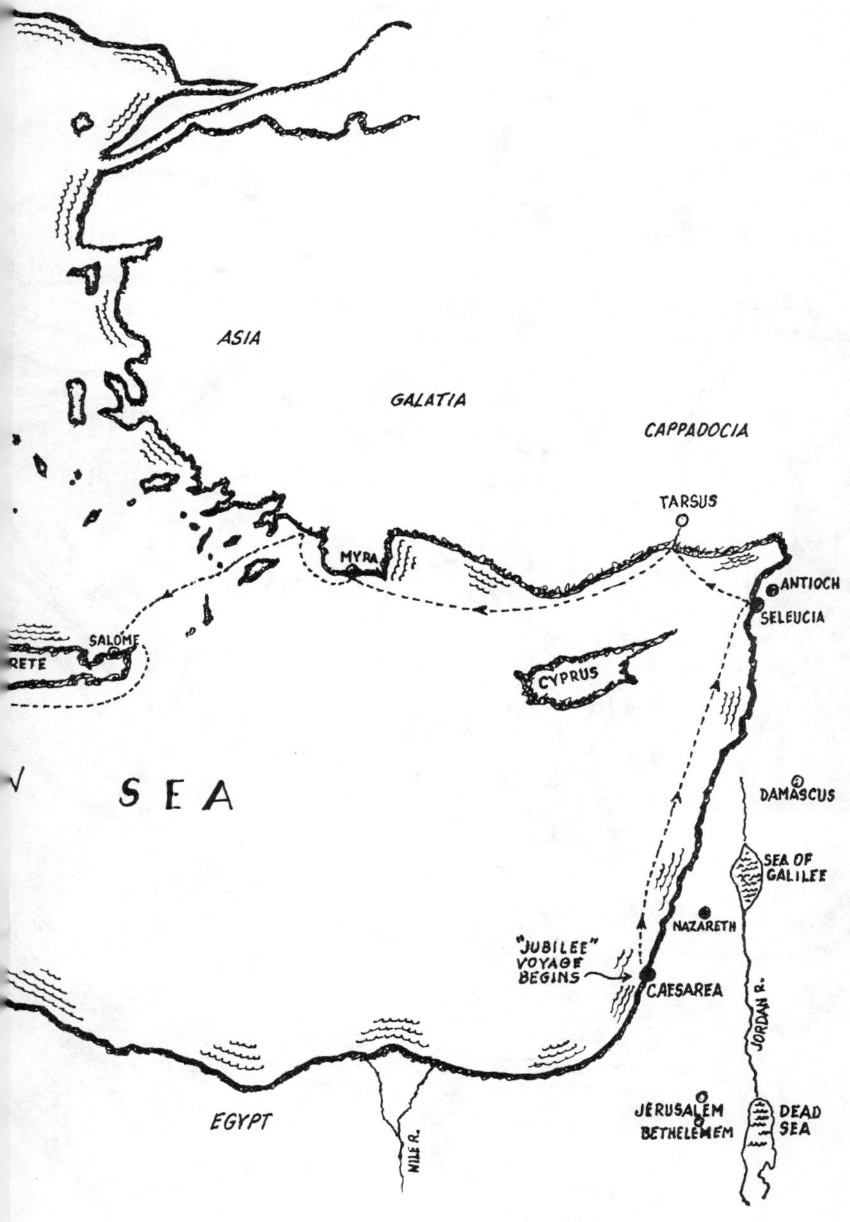
ASIA
GALATIA
CAPPADOCIA
TARSUS
MYRA
ANTIOCH
SELEUCIA
SALOME
RETE
CYPRUS
SEA
DAMASCUS
SEA OF GALILEE
NAZARETH
"JUBILEE" VOYAGE BEGINS
CAESAREA
JORDAN R.
EGYPT
JERUSALEM
BETHELEMEM
DEAD SEA
NILE R.

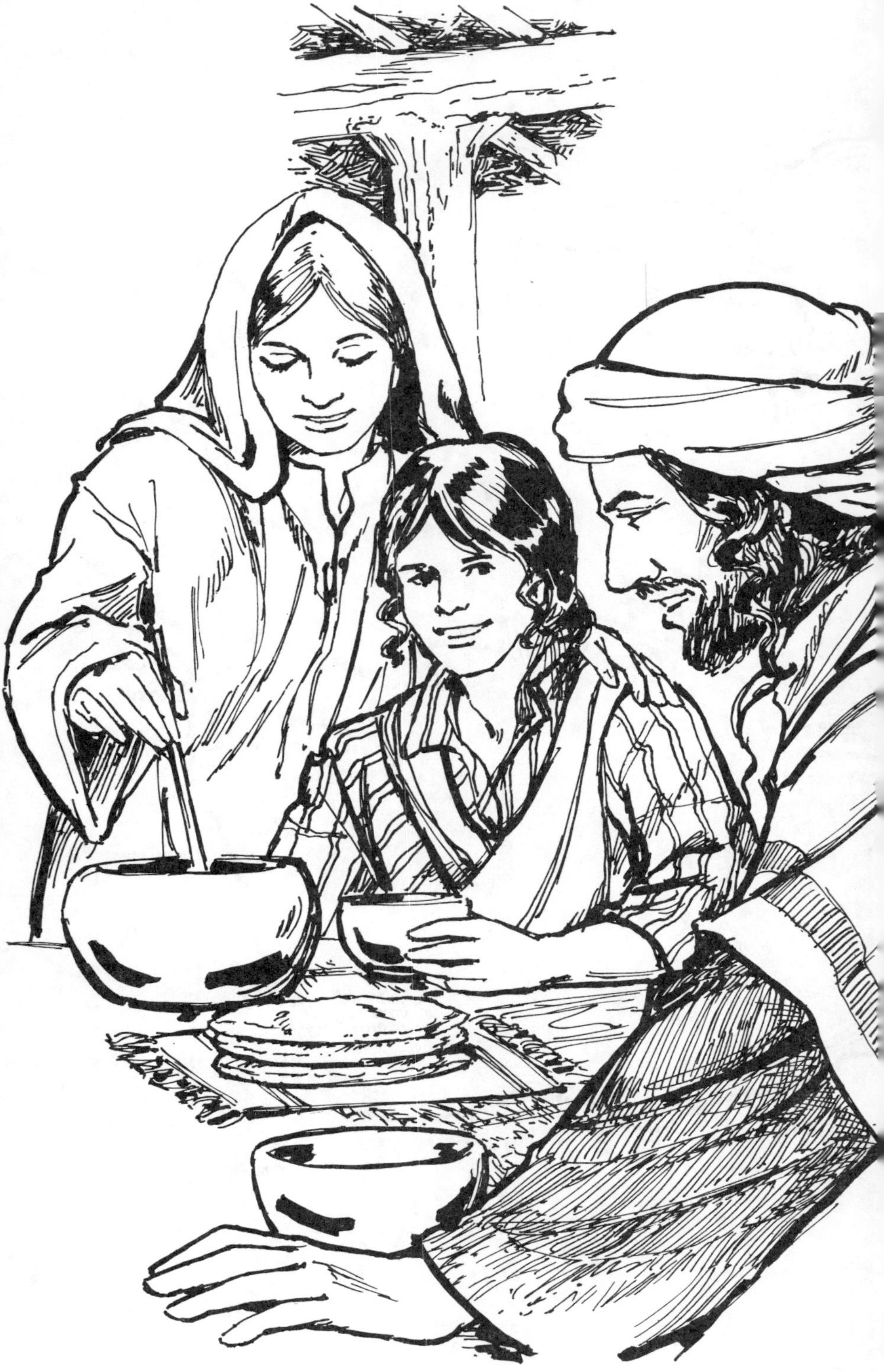

1

The Home at Nazareth

Jesus walked into the room and sat down at the table. In a glance he surveyed the one large room which had been his home for as long as he could remember. The room was dug out, really an extension of the side of a cave. The cave was as most other dwellings in the village. Here and there goatskin and woolen rugs covered the cave's earthen floor. The sleeping area was in the back of the room, sheepskin coverlets and hand-woven blankets neatly folded on the beds. On the right was the cooking area; a large, open earthen fireplace. Next to the fireplace was a free-standing cabinet containing pots and pans and dishes on its shelves; within its bottom drawers were the yarn and cloth and spindle his mother used for sewing and weaving. To his left was another wooden cabinet, attached by hooks to the soft limestone wall. In its drawers were the clothes of his father, mother, and his own. All these garments were made by his mother.

One drawer was very special; it contained scrolls on which were written the Holy Word. There were not many, but those that were there he knew so well that they were written more permanently in his heart than on the papyrus.

His mother stood by the fireplace, stirring the barley soup made with carrots and beans and peas from his father's garden. He could smell the barley bread which was baking in the oven. It was a warm, rich smell that meant for him a feeling of security, happiness, and peace. It was the smell of home, his home.

"Where is your father?" His mother looked at him with a smile.

"He will be here right away. He is washing up now."

As she returned to her cooking Jesus studied her more closely. She looked so young and, without a doubt, was the most beautiful woman he had ever seen. How old was mother now? Twenty-eight or twenty-nine? She did not show her years. She seemed to be more like the girls his own age whom he watched from the shop as they went back and forth to the well in the center of the village.

His mother was of medium height, her skin as fair as the olives on the trees in the grove. Her hair, held together by a scarf tied beneath her chin, was brown, but not so brown as the bark of the oak trees in the village square. It was more like the light brown of the sheaves of barley stacked in his father's yard after the harvest. Her eyes were light brown and in their depths shone a brilliant, sparkling light. He always felt that she said more with the look in her eyes than with her tongue.

People in the village said he looked like his mother. They could see something of her in the way he walked. They frequently commented on the tranquil beauty that shone in the eyes of both mother and son. His carriage and mannerisms, like hers, were marked by an indescribable nobility. Their friends and neighbors knew they were of royal blood, in spite of their poverty. The mother, Mary, and the father, Joseph, rightly claimed to be descendants of King David.

"Where is your father?" Mary asked again.

"He is coming. He just wanted to check on the chests we loaded into the carts."

Joseph entered through the large door, the only entrance and exit to the home. He was a tall man with square shoulders, large, muscular arms and hands that could tell anyone at a glance he was a craftsman. Behind his coal-black beard was an oval, oblong face that was weathered like the goatskin bag containing water that hung on the wall next to the door. His eyes were kindly and little lights danced in them when he smiled, which was very often. With his axe and plane, chisel and hammer, he made plows and yokes for the farmers of his own village, Nazareth, as well as the surrounding villages. Men throughout the area came to him, for they recognized the exceptional quality of his work. They knew Joseph was an honest man.

"There," he said, taking his usual place at the head of the table. "They are all neatly packed, crated, and covered with rags. No stone or jolt should scratch them now."

Joseph was talking about the eight cedar chests he had packed into the two carts. These chests were his pride and joy as a carpenter, a satisfaction the young man sitting next to him shared. These were not like the ordinary plows or yokes made from the wood of the local olive trees. These were chests he labored over whenever he could throughout the year. They would bring a price that would augment the paltry sums he received for the yokes from the nearby farmers. They meant a great deal in providing for the needs of his family. He very much needed this extra work in order to make ends meet.

"I really don't know what we would do if we did not have the order for these cedar chests," he spoke aloud but seemed rather to be thinking to himself. Mary, his wife, was setting the food on the table. After a pause the three bowed their heads and prayed aloud:

> Lord, your constant love reaches the heavens;
> your faithfulness extends to the skies.
> Your righteousness is towering like the mountains; your justice is like the depths of the sea.
> Men and animals are in your care.
> How precious, O God, is your constant love:
> We find protection under the shadow of your wings.
> We feast on the abundant food you provide; you let us drink from the river of your goodness.
> You are the source of all life, and because of your light we see the light.

Mary poured the soup, passing a bowl first to her husband and then to her son, Jesus. Mary served the small barley loaves of bread that she had just taken out of the oven.

Joseph was thinking of the kindness of his distinguished customer and what a boon he proved to be. Mary was thinking of the beauty of the cedar chests and the skills of her husband and young son in making these beautiful pieces of furniture. Jesus was thinking of the wood, the price his father paid for it at the market in Capernaum, and how it had been cut from the majestic cedars of distant Lebanon.

"It was good of Joseph of Arimathea to give us this order for the chests," Joseph said, this time looking directly at his wife.

"Indeed," Mary replied. "I wonder if he knows how much it means to us and how happy it makes you and Jesus when you have time to work with cedar instead of olive wood."

In his mind Joseph went back four years to that Passover in Jerusalem when they first met the merchant from Arimathea. Strange, he thought, that he stopped in the portico of the temple and asked us where we were from. Stranger still that he invited us to his tent to have an evening meal with him. He was such a young man, yet so worldly-wise.

That first night at supper in his tent Joseph told the family of Nazareth that he owned his own ship, anchored in the port of Caesarea. Most of the year he spent purchasing silks from Damascus, aromatic spices from Arabia and as far away as India, hand-carved statues of ivory from deepest Africa, and golden jewelry from Egypt. Once a year he sailed with his precious cargo to Rome and there realized a handsome profit. On his return voyage he brought back supplies for the Roman soldiers at the Herodian fortress in Caesarea.

"All in all," the merchant said, extending the bowl of dates and other fruits to the young Jesus, "it is a profitable business. In years to come I hope to be a wealthy man, a very wealthy man."

Jesus was only ten years old at this first meeting and he looked upon the young merchant with amazement. He liked Joseph of Arimathea and Joseph also took a liking to him. Before the one Joseph returned to his trading and the other Joseph started walking back with Jesus and Mary to the carpenter shop in Nazareth the two men struck a bargain. The former knew that he could sell cedar chests at a good price to Roman matrons. "If they were made," he said, "from the finest wood of the cedars of Lebanon."

That was four years ago. The agreement was a successful one. Each year the Arimathean urged Joseph to make more but he declined, for he felt he also had an obligation to supply the needs of his neighbors and friends who were farmers in Galilee. The merchant respected the carpenter's decision.

Each year Jesus looked forward to accompanying his parents to Jerusalem at Passover. Each year his heart leaped with joy as he entered the magnificent temple Herod the Great had rebuilt for the Jewish people. He loved to shout out with the men, women, and children in the caravan, "Shalom!" as they stood before the gates of Jerusalem, the city of peace. He loved this city deeply, even more than the other devout pilgrims in the hundreds of caravans that passed through these gates. As the family of Jesus entered the gate they sang with the others the words of David the King:

> How I rejoiced when they said to me,
> Let us go to the house of Yahweh:
> And now our feet are standing
> in your gateways, Jerusalem.

Each year they planned to see Joseph of Arimathea and dine with him. His mind returned to the present when Mary rose and brought a bowl of dates and pears from their garden. Joseph was stirred from his own thoughts by the action.

There was only silence, though. Silence which always seems much longer that it is. Sheep bleated in the corral outside. A fly buzzed over the open kettle on the hearth. Finally, Jesus spoke.

"Mother, may I go with Joseph of Arimathea?"

Mary knew this question would be asked sooner or later this night. She looked lovingly and intently at her son.

"My son," she softly replied, "you are so young." In a mother's eyes a son always seems to be a child.

"I am fourteen," he replied with equal calmness. "You know, mother, according to the Law I am a man."

She and Joseph had talked many nights before sleep about the Arimathean's offer to take Jesus with him on a journey to Rome. It was an opportunity, they knew, but it was also dangerous. Mary could not deny that legally Jesus was a young man. Yet, who would know what dangers might beset Jesus on so distant a trip. The remembrance of their losing him in the temple two years ago sent sharp pains to her heart. She looked to Joseph.

"Jesus is right, Mary." He looked tenderly at his wife. "He is a man and I know he does a man's work. In no time he will even surpass me in our trade."

"But do we know that Joseph will take good care of Jesus?" She was hedging now. She knew the merchant would.

"He promised," Joseph reassured her, "that he would look after Jesus as if he were his own son."

"This is not just a two- or three-day journey to Caesarea." Mary was thinking out loud. "That I would think should be enough the first year. But Joseph, we are talking about Rome! That will be months and months!"

"I know. But you must admit it is a great opportunity for Jesus."

Mary was beginning to retreat in her own mind. She thought as she had frequently in the past that perhaps Jesus must be, as he once said, "about his father's business." Who was she to stand in the way?

"I am not afraid, Mother," Jesus said to calm her. "You know, I am never alone."

And Mary said, "Then you must go. I am glad that you will be with Joseph of Arimathea."

Jesus was delighted and he touched his mother's arm gently. Those little lights in Joseph's eyes were dancing as a broad smile covered his face. Mary looked up, glancing first at her husband and then at her son. A soft smile crossed her face.

"Now, that's decided," said Joseph. "That is good." He knew somehow it would turn out this way and Mary would accede to the merchant's offer. The family bowed their heads in a prayer of thanksgiving. In her own heart Mary added, "Be it done unto me, O Lord, according to thy word."

Joseph rose and started for the door. Over his shoulder he said, "Jesus, go to Uncle Cleophas and ask for the two burros. We will need them here for our departure before dawn. Tell him I will be along with the goat and sheep later."

Jesus ran down the winding cobblestone street. The sun was lowering in the west and he hoped he and his cousins, Simon and Jude, would be able to climb the hills before it disappeared. He hurriedly greeted the neighbors sitting in front of their homes, enjoying the evening breezes and reviewing the events of what was for them an eventless day.

One old man, watching Jesus hurrying by, turned to his wife. "Jesus must be going with Joseph to Caesarea. He seems happy." Little did he or anyone else in Nazareth know yet that Jesus was going on a journey with a destination much more important than Caesarea.

In a matter of minutes Jesus returned with the two burros and two young men about his own age. Simon and Jude greeted Mary and Joseph and were as much in a hurry as Jesus to climb the hills before the sun set. They had done it so often in the past that they knew every footpath, almost every rock, along the way. After they had helped Jesus hitch the burrows to the carts the three young men were hurrying along the narrow streets leading to the foot of the mountain. They did not tarry at the village square where women were still drawing water from the well.

Although the three had stood on the top of the mountain so many times that they had lost count, they still approached each trip as a new adventure. They no longer knew if it was their friendship, or the view, or the exercise of climbing the mountain that attached them to this ritualistic endeavor. Perhaps the panorama from the height afforded them the opportunity to dream dreams that little Nazareth could neither offer nor afford. Perhaps on this mountain, too, they felt a sense of stability and security that every man, no matter what his age, needed for peace and serenity. In their way their frequent visits took on the nature of a pilgrimage. More than once as they stood speechless and breathless on the summit one or the other would repeat the words of the prophet Joel they had learned in school: "Your old men shall dream dreams and your young men see visions."

This evening, however, Simon and Jude could not wait to reach the top. Jesus had told them he had something very special to tell them. They were anxious to hear for the two always looked to Jesus as their leader.

They wore red caftans as all other young men in the village. Their homespun tunics were made by their mothers, woven from the wool shorn from the sheep in their little pastures. Over their tunics Jesus and his cousins wore loose-fitting jackets, for they knew it would be cool when they descended from the mountain.

They laughed when Jude told about the silly young girl who fell in the well that day with the women and girls standing there shrieking and crying for help. Her father came to the rescue and, with the girl still dripping wet, spanked her in the presence of all.

"You would think he would have been overjoyed that she did not drown," Jesus said.

"But some fathers are like that, you know," was Simon's philosophical comment.

They talked, too, about the beautiful chests Joseph and Jesus had completed. Simon told Jesus he should be proud that he helped his father make them. Jesus said nothing. Suddenly they stood on the summit of the mountain which served as a great protective mantle for the little village that tumbled down its southeast side. They looked back with satisfaction at the ascent they had made.

Nazareth lay at their feet, its white stucco houses and doorways peeping out from the greenery that surrounded them. Here and there purple bougainvillea climbed along the side of a house with some of the branches reaching over its roof. The village was encompassed by green olive trees and green shrubbery. The greenery made the white of the houses more pronounced so that travelers and visitors called Nazareth "the white village."

"It looks like a large white rose," said Jude, "just beginning to open its petals." All three loved this village very much for it was home — family and friends, school and synagogue, workshops and gardens. They knew its every lane and all its people. The sights and sounds of Jerusalem that they heard and saw each year at Passover were enough to keep them talking for weeks, even months. But Nazareth was closer to the heart.

They looked to the horizon and all around and saw an endless sky, quickly changing from saffron and orange to dark blue to purple. To the south lay other villages and other people, not unlike their own. They pointed out Cana in the distance. South and west lay the magnificent Plain of

Esdralon with its endless acres of wheat waving gently in the evening breeze. To the east they picked out the mountains of Gilead and Moab, silent sentinels of the Jordan Valley and Sea of Galilee. And around to the west was the majestic Mount Tabor. They often said that someday they would go there to climb its heights.

Turning south they surveyed the plain of Jezreel dotted with villages like Naim and Endor Lego which Jesus often visited with his father. In the distance they sighted the mountains of Samaria gradually drifting into the long bluish range of Carmel that dropped into the sea. They turned north and wondered again, as they always did, at the might and power of Mount Hermon whose snow-covered peaks pierced the sky. After standing silently in awe for several minutes Simon turned to Jesus, "Now tell us what great secret you have."

"I am going on a long journey tomorrow," he replied, simply and directly.

"Oh, we already knew that," said Jude. "We figured out that Joseph would be taking you with him one of these years to Caesarea."

"You figured right, Jude," Jesus smiled, "but you didn't figure far enough."

"Then just where are you going?"

"To Rome."

"To Rome!"

The sun had fallen off the edge of the world and into the sea. The brothers looked at each other and then at Jesus. They were stunned by the strange news.

"To Rome!" Simon whispered. Silence covered the three with its cloak of wonderment. A young man from Nazareth would go to Rome!

In silence the three walked down the mountainside to their homes. As they came to Jesus' home, Mary and Joseph were sitting by the doorway.

"Is it true?" Simon asked incredulously, looking at Mary.

"Yes, Simon. Tomorrow morning Jesus leaves with Joseph on his journey to Rome."

"And now," said Joseph, "to bed."

* * * * * *

The family in Nazareth was up and quietly moving about while the morning star was still shining brightly in the eastern sky. Each was occupied with tasks preparing for the journey to Caesarea.

"Jesus," Mary spoke softly, "be sure to be obedient and helpful to Joseph of Arimathea. He is showing all of us a great kindness in taking you with him to Rome."

Joseph entered the house. He had finished packing the carts, placing his own belongings and two bedrolls in one of the wagons. He had planned they would sleep under the stars in the pass of the Carmel Mountains to give the burros and themselves a night's rest. They would easily reach the port of Caesarea before nightfall the following day.

"Come, Jesus, we must leave." Joseph turned to Mary, embraced her, and said, "I shall be back, God willing, in three days, although it will be late. Have no fear. Cleophas will look after you and Simon and Jude will do the chores. God keep you in his care."

"And God be with you on your journey, my husband."

Jesus came over, embraced and kissed his mother. "Do not fear, mother. You know I am safe in God's hands."

Mary looked lovingly into the eyes of her son and pronounced over him the blessing that God gave Moses: "May Yahweh bless you and keep you. May Yahweh let his face shine on you and be gracious to you. May Yahweh uncover his face to you and bring you peace."

Joseph closed the door behind him. Mary sat at the table, listening to the burros whine and the wooden wheels of the carts screech over the stones on the road. She listened and prayed until she heard no more sound. In the stillness of the early morn she prayed for the safe return of her son, her husband, and the good merchant, Joseph of Arimathea.

* * * * * *

Father and son led the burros as quietly as possible through the dusty streets of the village. They did not want to disturb the sleep of friends and neighbors. Soon they were on the narrow, winding road that led down the hillside toward the floor of the valley. There were neither walls nor gate to the village, for Nazareth was much too small and unimportant to demand any kind of defense. It was off the main route that crossed from north to south through Galilee. The dwellings soon disappeared into the side of the mountain that Jesus and his cousins had climbed the night before. Joseph and Jesus then passed an occasional dwelling almost buried in olive groves until they came to the common pasture lands of the village. Jesus looked back for one last look at this hidden little village that was home for him and contained so many happy memories of his boyhood.

"My son," Joseph broke the silence, "we will have a long journey and a hard one before us and will have to keep a fast pace if we are to meet Joseph as scheduled tomorrow evening. We need not worry, though, for God is with us and will protect us all along the way."

Father and son wended their way along the narrow, dirty roads through the hillsides and valleys of Galilee. The darkness of night was being conquered again by the first streaks of gray along the tops of the Galilean hills. From time to time the stillness was broken by one of the many little birds nested in the olive trees who wanted to prove to his fellows and the world that he was an early riser and believed in the old saying that the early bird gets the worm. As if that made him a better bird! Jesus wondered if birds are like human beings who think they are better because they rise earlier. For his part, he did not really believe in that old saying about the early bird the old men in the village liked to quote.

With the dawning Jesus became more alert. He deeply loved his native land. Its hills afforded continuing variety as the sun-made shadows danced along their sides. Its little valleys nestled among the hills provided rich, green pasture land for the sheep and goats whose owners lived in the little villages perched along the hillsides. This hilly land provided for him and his family and neighbors all the necessities of life. Others might look down their noses at this rustic, rural country he called his home. Here he and his family and neighbors were safe and secure from the tumults of Jerusalem, the tyranny of Herod, and the political power of Rome.

"We are now coming to Sapporis," Joseph called back to his son who was leading the other burro and wagon. "Here we will meet the main road that will lead us to Megiddo and Caesarea."

"I have never been in Sapporis, father," Jesus called back. He had often accompanied his father to such towns as Naim, Cana, Magdala, and even Capernaum when he brought his finished yokes or tables or chairs to his customers.

"Your mother told you this town was the home of your grandmother, Anne," Joseph called back. "I have never come here because no one ever asked me to work for him."

The young man's thoughts turned to his grandmother, Anne, whom he never knew. He wondered what his grandfather, Joachim, did for a living. His mother spoke very little about them because, as she told him, she was taken from them when only three years old and offered as a servant-maid in the great temple of Jerusalem. She returned to Nazareth when she was twelve and then lived with her cousin Miriam. By that time both her parents had died.

In Sapporis the two carpenters turned south. They were now on a broader and smoother road. The traveling was easier. They stopped at the well in the village only long enough to refresh themselves and the burros. The sun had peeked over the mountains and bathed the well and the houses of Sapporis in a mellow golden hue.

"Our next stop," Joseph said, "will be Megiddo. We will be crossing the Plain of Esdralon and you will notice the many fields of barley and wheat. The farmers here are much wealthier than they are in Nazareth."

Jesus did not reply. He was thinking of the time that he walked behind his father when he was only four years old and had sown his own seeds of wheat in their little garden. He recalled the joy in his mother's eyes when he ran into the house at the time of the harvest and placed in her lap the sheaves of ripened wheat that he had planted with his own hands. In his mind's eye he saw how his mother kneaded the grains of wheat, grinding them between the two flat stones and making them into flour for bread. He continually gazed at the fields of waving wheat and barley along both sides of the road. He wondered how many more times in his life he would cross this rich and beautiful Plain of Esdralon.

The sun was rising higher and its rays were casting shadows that were playing hide-and-seek among the fields. Not even a puff of a cloud was in the sky or on the horizon. The two travelers maintained a quick, steady pace and spoke very little.

Joseph was wondering about his son and what new and strange adventures lay before him. He did not worry, though, because he firmly believed in the Providence of the great God and repeated to himself the words he often heard in the synagogue on the Sabbath: "Those who trust in Yahweh are like Mount Zion, unshakable, standing for ever." Joseph himself was just that kind of a man. This journey, he thought, was in God's hands, just as that earlier journey into Egypt that he and Mary and their son had made many years before.

By now the sun stood in the middle of the sky and the travelers were entering the outskirts of Megiddo. "We will stop here," said Joseph, "and give the animals and ourselves a rest. Draw some water from the well and I will lead the burros to that grove of olive trees over there. We can eat the lunch your mother prepared and feed the burros."

Jesus took an empty goatskin, filled it with water and was back at his father's side in a few minutes. Joseph had taken feed for the burros from the cart. Jesus poured water into an earthen pot and set it before the animals. He returned, took the wooden box, spread out a napkin and set the food on it. Joseph came with the goatskin filled with wine. Together they recited a psalm and Joseph blessed the food.

As they lunched Joseph told his son what he knew about Megiddo. "It is a very ancient city," he said, "going so far back into history that no one can recall when or how it began. The narrow pass in the Carmel mountain range has made this city very important. The pass is the main link between east and west. Traders from Egypt and Syria, and thousands of soldiers throughout the centuries, have climbed up and down that pass."

"The rabbi taught us the king of Megiddo was one of the thirty-one kings Joshua conquered," Jesus added as he broke another piece of bread and placed cheese on it.

"You would not remember," Joseph continued, "but this was the road your mother and I, with you as a baby, took when we left Egypt and returned to Nazareth." Joseph again fell into silence. Jesus wondered, as he often did, why his father was such a quiet man. The burros were finished with their feeding; so were Joseph and Jesus.

"Come," Joseph was rising, "let us be on our way."

The two carpenters, the two burros, the two carts laden with eight fine cedar chests, hurried out of Megiddo on their way to the pass.

For what seemed a terribly long time the afternoon sun filled the travelers with a warmth that was soothing. Not suddenly, but almost instantly, the orange sun dropped behind the hills and the cypress, pines, and brush took on a bluish-gray color in the lengthening shadows. The two were in the sloping hill countryside, beginning their ascent to the pass. They had not met any other individuals or groups of travelers for a long time. The birds were fluttering in the branches of the trees and bushes, bedding down for the night. A hush enveloped them and the earth surrendered the heat the sun's rays had loaned it only a few hours before.

"We shall soon be at the resting-place, Jesus," said Joseph. "I hope you are not too tired."

"I am tired, father," Jesus replied. "I suspect the burros are also tired. I will be glad when we stop and have something to eat."

They trudged on, climbing the slope. Jesus turned when he heard voices in the distance behind him. He could not see plainly enough to determine who the group of seven or eight people might be. He thought of his mother. She must be lonely preparing her evening meal without Joseph and him. He wondered, too, about his grandmother, Anne, and what kind of woman she must have been like. He recalled, too, that one of King David's wives was from Carmel; her name was Abigail and called by the sacred writer "the wife of Nabal from Carmel." As he gazed about the slopes so verdant in their spring greenery he remembered that Isaiah wrote about "the splendor of Carmel." Even the mournful Jeremiah wrote about "Carmel high above the sea."

Jesus glanced back again. Now he could clearly see the group approaching from the rear. They were soldiers. Eight Roman soldiers! A sense of fear took hold of him. He had only seen solders before when he went with his father and mother to Jerusalem.

"Father! There are Roman soldiers behind us!"

"I know, do not be afraid," Joseph spoke calmly, reassuring the troubled Jesus. "They cannot harm us. We have done no wrong."

Jesus knew that; but somehow it did not matter. He knew he must like them as men, but he did not like them as soldiers. Yahweh did not create men to fight against one another!

"It may be a blessing for us, Jesus, that they are here."

"Why is that, father?"

"Most probably they will also camp overnight at the resting-place before going on to Caesarea in the morning. Their presence will protect us from any thieves that may be on the prowl during the night." Joseph nudged the burros with the carts to the side of the road to make room for the soldiers to pass. Jesus picked up his pace to come side by side with Joseph.

The soldiers approached. They were not marching, just strolling, and seemed to be swaggering. They were loud and boisterous, letting out shrill guffaws and wild, animal-like yells.

"Shalom," Joseph greeted them calmly and respectfully.

"You going to the resting-place?" One who walked straighter and more firmly than the others asked.

"Yes, sir."

"So are we. You best hurry along." The soldier's companions looked haughtily and disdainfully at the two travelers.

"You're Galileans?" Another soldier paused a moment to ask the question.

"Yes, sir," said Joseph. "We are from Nazareth."

"Where's that?"

"Near Capernaum and the Sea of Galilee."

"I could tell that by the way you talk." The soldier spit on the ground.

"You look more miserable than synagogue mice," he spoke as if talking to himself. "Why do the gods let riff-raff like this clutter up the earth!"

"You will be safe at the resting-place," the first soldier said. "Try to stay close behind us. It's getting dark."

"Thank you, sir," Jesus replied this time. He detected a note of humanity, almost kindness, in the soldier's voice. With that the boisterous, drinking, hard-headed soldiers passed them by.

* * * * * *

The burros were tethered to a tree in a far corner of the resting place, which was no more than a dusty patch of earth surrounded by olive trees. Jesus immediately realized why the spot was made a resting place. At its entrance was a well that weary travelers used for washing and bathing. He was unrolling the sleeping mats on the ground when Joseph returned from the carts where he placed the box of food Mary had prepared for them.

"Tomorrow's journey will be easy, Jesus." Joseph stretched his tired body out on the mat. "Tomorrow we will descend about two thousand feet from the pass and then follow the coastal road to Caesarea."

"Do you like Caesarea, father?" Jesus sprawled on his mat, resting his elbow on the ground with his head cupped in his hand. He noticed the sounds were dying down around them and even the soldiers were quiet. They must be asleep, he thought.

"No, Jesus, I do not. For that matter I don't think any of our countrymen do. A long time ago, when it was one of our cities, it was called the Tower of Straton. But Herod made it more like a city in Greece, they say, even if it took only twelve years to build."

"Why do our people despise Herod so much?"

"He was cruel, a tyrant. Because of him we had to become exiles in Egypt, you know. He made life very difficult for us, Jesus. I think our people will suffer a great deal more because of him. He favored the Romans more than the Jews, you know. Now, let us say a prayer, and then to sleep." The two rose, bowed their heads and together recited another song of David:

> Yahweh is king, robed in majesty,
> Yahweh is robed in power,
> He wears it like a belt.
> You have made the world firm, unshakable;
> Your throne has stood since then,
> You existed from the first, Yahweh.
> Yahweh, the rivers raise,
> The rivers raise their voices,
> The rivers raise their thunders;
> Greater than the voice of ocean,
> Transcending the waves of the sea,
> Yahweh reigns transcendent in the heights.
> Your decrees will never alter;
> Holiness will distinguish your house,
> Yahweh, for ever and ever.

The two stood briefly in silence, then Joseph embraced the young man and blessed him.

"Now, to sleep," said Joseph. "The morning will come before you know it."

"Good night, my father."

"Good night, Jesus."

But Jesus laid awake, watching the stars, sparkling and glistening in the sky like sequins shining on the robes of the Syrian merchant they passed along the way. He listened to the grunts and groans from the two burros and other animals tied to the trees around the resting-place. He wondered where these twenty or twenty-five people in the resting place were all going. Some of them looked like family groups going on a visit to relatives or friends. Others, like themselves, looked like merchants, or perhaps salesmen. The soldiers he knew were going to Caesarea. He asked himself if they were also lonesome for their homes. He knew at least one of them did not like Galileans. Why, he thought, was that? He knew he should not disturb his father by asking the question that was forming on his lips. He fell asleep wondering, just wondering.

2

The Terrible Palace of Herod

"Merchant of Arimathea! When do you sail?" Joseph knew that voice well. It was Philip, the harbor master, calling from his office at the foot of the pier. Philip was an officious man, much more conscious of his importance than anyone else. From experience Joseph knew it was prudent to treat this official kindly and with the deference he enjoyed so much.

"I plan to sail at full tide tomorrow morning," he answered as he walked into the lean-to that was Philip's office. He knew Philip was prepared to besiege him with a battery of questions whose answers he would neatly record in quadruplicate to satisfy Roman bureaucracy. He knew, too, that Philip fitted neatly into this machinery for it gave him a sense of his own importance. No one dared call him what he really was, a minor functionary on a very low rung of the Roman ladder.

"What delays you?" Philip grunted more than asked. "I have a wife and daughters at home waiting for our evening meal. I cannot be chained to this desk all night."

"My ship is almost completely loaded, the sailors are already in the galley and the captain is ready to sail at a moment's notice." Joseph spoke slowly and politely. He also knew that Philip could make things difficult if he wanted. "I am waiting only for one passenger and a small cargo of eight cedar chests."

"When will the passenger be here?" Philip already began filling out the questionnaire for he knew the answers without asking.

"He should be here shortly, in the company of his father, who is a carpenter. As a matter of fact, I expect them any moment. But they are coming from Nazareth which, you know, is a long journey."

"From Nazareth!" Philip scoffed. "What good can come from so miserable a village! Who is this passenger?" By nature Philip was inquisitive, a quality which no doubt prompted the authorities to employ him for this perfunctory task.

"He is a young man by the name of Jesus," the merchant replied. "I came to know him and his parents four years ago at Passover. This year I asked his parents' permission to let me take him with me to Rome. He may be interested in being apprenticed in my firm, I hope. For some reason I am strangely attracted to him. He is, as you will see, Philip, a young man of exceptional quality."

"We shall see," said Philip, brushing the subject off like a speck of dust on his sleeve. "If that is all, we can finish filling out these forms. Then, thank God, I can get home to my wife and family."

Without being offered a seat, Joseph remained standing next to the harbor master. Philip continued filling out the forms, muttering to himself as he did. Joseph knew it would be some time before being asked a question or two but knew it best to remain patiently standing. That increased Philip's satisfaction with the importance of his job.

Joseph glanced about this city that he did not particularly like. He preferred Joppa, the ancient port, where he used to go in the company of his father. That was a Jewish city and its citizens shared his religion. It was a friendly city where almost everyone greeted you with "Shalom!" Of course, business is business, there as elsewhere, but the business carried out in Joppa was overlaid with religious traditions centuries old, dictated and prescribed by the ancestors of his people.

"What is the name of your ship?" Philip interrupted Joseph's thoughts.

"*Jubilee*," Joseph replied, "in honor of our religious festival."

Philip did not answer. He made himself appear extremely busy by merely writing the name of the ship in the blank on the form. Strange, thought Joseph, this was his eighth journey and each time Philip asked the same question. He let Philip return to his task of filling in the blanks. This was Philip's bread and butter. No man should begrudge or deprive another his livelihood.

Joseph looked around this new city, casting his glances from north to south and as far east as the eye could see. It was only thirty-four years old and every edifice in it, including the walls with their circular towers, was made of gleaming white marble. Herod the Great built it to serve as the principal seaport of his kingdom. He named it in honor of his patron, Caesar Augustus. No doubt, thought Joseph,

Herod was a great builder, for he also rebuilt the temple in Jerusalem. But they also whispered that he was an idolator and had built secret shrines to his own false gods. And he was not a Jew, just an Idumean upstart.

This was the first and primary reason for Joseph's dislike for this city. Herod could, indeed, build such monuments but the cost was supplied by the heavy taxation he imposed upon all the citizens of the kingdom. The Jews still turn and spit on the ground at the mere mention of his name, and he had been dead now for ten years. But one must at least give him credit for building the only safe and secure port in his country. Joppa was a dangerous, treacherous harbor, constantly being buffeted by southerly gales and storms.

But this city was not like any other in Palestine. It was a Roman, not Jewish, city. Its apartments, offices, and shops, its amphitheater, and even Herod's own ostentatious palace were all built in the decadent architectural style employed by the Romans throughout the empire. The keen observer could immediately see that the style had lost the classical purity of earlier Roman architecture and did not even approach the graceful elegance of Grecian architecture.

Herod's palace was immense, perched on a hillside overlooking both the harbor and the city. Its size was but another indication of its vulgarity. Its gardens were more magnificent than all the other gardens in the city, and there were many. But the beauty of the gardens and their many fountains crumbled into dust when one thought of the misery of the slaves who were forced to tend them. The palace proclaimed that Herod wanted to be more Roman than Jewish, and that was another reason why the Jews detested him. The palace represented Herod's tyranny and debauchery and the people still argued which of the two was his greater vice.

Herod's greatest perversity, however, was not the fact that he named the city in honor of Augustus but dared to build a temple overlooking the harbor to deify the emperor. The Jews of the city revolted when Herod installed in this temple the statues of the goddess of Rome and the divine Octavian Caesar. That, thought Joseph, was the most despicable and sinful act of this terribly cruel and loathsome man who slaughtered even members of his own family on the least suspicion. With cynical impunity he dared to mock the God of Israel who proclaimed to Moses on Sinai: "I am the Lord your God; you shall not have strange gods before me."

"How many members of your crew?" Philip looked up from the forms on the desk.

"Pardon me?"

"How many crew members?" Philip showed irritation by the gruffness of his voice.

"The captain, the first mate, thirty sailors, a cook, my steward, and the young man from Nazareth as a passenger."

"And yourself?"

"Of course."

Philip went back to his forms. Joseph knew the interrogation was finished and knew, too, that Philip was able to answer most of the questions without even asking. The transaction would be completed when he paid the fee. He began opening his purse to dig out fifty drachmas.

"And the fee?" asked Joseph.

"Sixty drachmas."

"It was only fifty-six months ago."

"I know," answered Philip, "but everything has gone up. How do you expect the government to maintain so magnificent a harbor..."

"I know, I know," Joseph interrupted. He knew better than to argue with a government official; you never win. Joseph counted out the sixty drachmas into Philip's waiting hand.

"And two for you and your good family." Joseph was tying the strings on his purse.

"Thank you kindly," said Philip. "May our great Yahweh reward you and grant you a safe journey." He busied himself cleaning off the top of his desk, filing scrolls in pigeon holes and pushing other papers into the drawer. Joseph stood outside the little office as Philip closed and locked the door behind him. "Who is your agent in Rome?" he asked.

"A good man, a God-fearing pagan by the name of Urban. Have you ever heard of him?"

"Heard of him!" Philip's face lighted up. "Indeed, so, I have met him twice when he passed through this port. You are fortunate. He is most honest and observes our Law."

"And who is your steward? I know, I know, I wrote his name down but I forgot."

"His name is Nicodemus, a young man from Jerusalem." Joseph was looking searchingly along the promenade that circled the harbor. "He comes from a wealthy family of merchants in Jerusalem and his father asked me to take him on to give him some experience. I was glad to do so. You know, it helps to have good connections."

"How well I know!" Philip exclaimed. "How else do you think I got this job?"

"There!" cried Joseph, pointing to the southern portion of the promenade. "There! I see them now. The two carpenters from Nazareth!" He quickly left Philip and strode along the pier to meet them.

"Shalom!" said the merchant.

"Shalom!" replied the carpenter, embracing his friend. Jesus also extended the traditional greeting and embrace.

"Nicodemus!" Joseph cried to the young man standing on the prow of the boat, "bring four sailors to carry these beautiful chests to the ship's hold." Nicodemus shouted his reply to Joseph and his orders to four sailors, then disappeared.

The merchant inquired about their journey and expressed his pleasure that all went well along the way. He told Joseph he was confident all the time that Mary would consent to Jesus' going on the voyage to Rome.

Philip approached the threesome. Some people called

him nosy, but Philip always explained it was in the line of duty. Joseph introduced the Nazareans to Philip.

"It is my deep pleasure," Philip said and bowed slightly. "This man from Arimathea has been telling me about you all day. I see," rubbing his hands over the top of one of the chests, "that Joseph is well aware of the high quality of your craftsmanship. These are remarkable, exquisite pieces." Philip uttered the words carefully, as one who knew — or at least should know — the value of the merchandise that passed through the harbor.

"Young man," Philip turned to Jesus, "you are fortunate to be traveling with Joseph to Rome. Not everyone your age has such an opportunity."

Jesus looked at Philip. "You know," said Jesus, "our sacred writer has given us these words: 'Rejoice in your youth, you who are young; let your heart give you joy in your young days. Follow the promptings of your heart and the desires of your eyes.'"

"That same writer, I believe," said Philip, "also wrote, 'However great the number of the years a man may live, let him enjoy them all, and yet remember that dark days will be many.'"

"I am sure, sir," Jesus spoke directly to Philip, "that dark days will surely come to both of us."

Nicodemus approached with the sailors and Joseph again introduced the two carpenters. Nicodemus was only two years older than Jesus. He departed with the sailors, leading the burros and the carts to the ship's gangplank.

"Come, now," Joseph said, "let us all go to the ship for dinner. You travelers will have a chance to wash up and I know our cook will be ready for us. Philip, come along. We would be happy to have you dine with us."

"Thank you," Philip said, "but my wife and daughters are waiting. I have been honored to meet you two carpenters. Young man, I do hope we meet again someday."

"I am sure," Jesus replied as he looked deeply into Philip's eyes, "I am sure that we will."

Philip embraced all three and invoked on them the ancient blessing of Moses. He walked away, wondering what adventures awaited this young man on his journey.

* * * * * *

The cook was removing the plates and bowls from the table. It had been the finest dinner Jesus had ever eaten: fresh fish from the sea, fresh vegetables and fruits from the hillside, breads and pastries whose names he did not know, and sweet white Syrian wine. He wondered how many people ate so sumptuously. All during the dinner the merchant was asking them questions about how long it took to make a chest, where Joseph had purchased the cedar wood, what their shop in Nazareth was like, and how did Jesus enjoy the journey to Caesarea.

"Now," said the merchant, "Nicodemus will show you the deck and where your bedroll will be laid out for the night, Jesus. It will be a short night for we cast off as the tide goes out before dawn. Your father and I will join you in a few minutes."

Nicodemus was already on his feet and Jesus followed him from his specially arranged dining area to another corner of the deck. Side by side they stood in silence.

Jesus had often thought the most beautiful sight he had ever seen was the moon and stars dancing on the waters of the Sea of Galilee when he went with his father to Capernaum. That view paled in comparison to the one he now beheld. The lights of Caesarea climbed up the hillsides in the east like so many glittering stars reaching for the sky. The new moon and stars in the west pierced the darkness but were so far away they cast no light on the water. At one point it looked as if the Big Dipper was falling into the sea.

"Joseph wanted to conclude his business with your father," Nicodemus was saying, conscious of the fact that he was interrupting Jesus' reverie about the stars and the city and the skies and the sea. "They will be with us very soon. I hope you will not be lonesome, Jesus?"

"Oh! I will not be lonesome," Jesus replied. "I know there will be many things to do. I am grateful that Joseph invited me on this journey."

"Over there," Nicodemus said, pointing his right hand to the sky, "are the stars Castor and Pollux. They are the stars by which navigators steer their ships at night. The pagans have made gods out of them for ships would not be able to sail at night if we did not see them. Those of us who are true believers, though, call them the twin lamps the angels hold to guide us on our way."

"You will learn much about the stars in the coming weeks, Jesus," said the merchant as he and Joseph stood beside the two young men.

"My son," said the carpenter as he put his arm around Jesus' shoulder, "you will be respectful and obedient to our friend Joseph on this journey."

"You know I will, my father."

"That I know, but it will help me to reassure your mother when I return home."

"And you may tell your wife, Mary, that I shall protect Jesus as if he were my very own son," the merchant said as added reassurance. "And now, to bed. We rise before dawn on the morrow."

Jesus was already awake when he heard the first mate sound the ship's bell. His heart beat rapidly with excitement as any teenager's heart would beat on so momentous a day. The April moon hung low above the horizon and the polar star was brightly twinkling. Suddenly all hands on deck came to life, hurriedly rolling their sleeping mats and pulling their sandals over their bare feet. He quickly followed their example. What appeared to him as utter confusion was in reality each man hurriedly taking his station and assigned task. The captain insisted on leaving the harbor before the tide went out, even though it was only three feet high. His father and the merchant were suddenly at his side.

"I must leave you now, my son," Joseph said. "Be sure to show your gratitude to our friend Joseph because of his great goodness to all of us."

"I will, father, as best I can. I shall miss you and mother very much, but I will not be homesick."

"Greet Mary for me," said the merchant. "Tell her not to worry. God willing, Jesus should be home with you in Nazareth by the time of the high holydays in fall."

Joseph was gazing tenderly at his son. When the merchant finished, Joseph embraced Jesus but said not a word. He turned and the merchant accompanied him to the gangplank. The two talked briefly, embraced, and the carpenter began his long and lonely journey home. Jesus stood watching from the deck as his father walked the length of the pier, watched him along the broad boulevard that circled the harbor, watched him until he disappeared in the morning darkness. Jesus thought of his native village, his friends, his mother, and all the people and places that were dear to him at home.

3

The Meeting of Two Worlds

The *Jubilee* grunted, groaned, and lunged forward. Jesus was jolted from his reverie. He became aware of sailors swarming about the deck, the yelling and shouting of the first mate to the stevedores on the pier, the lighted fire in the prow of the boat, and by now the constant clanging of the ship's bell. It was all amazing to him, new and adventurous. The largest body of water he had ever seen was the Sea of Galilee; the largest boats were the dories a small handful of fishermen rowed by hand and the gaily decorated pleasure crafts of the tourists at Tiberias. The constant thump-thump-thump was a puzzlement to him. He discovered its origin only when he saw a sailor beating on what looked like a hollow drum as his shipmates manned the oars in unison.

The first slim ribbon of dawn was outlining the uneven

hills and mountains in the east. Jesus recognized the highest peak of Mount Carmel in the distance. Slowly the light was peeping over the hills, changing the black-blue of the water to a purple with a tint of green. The ship was a mile or so out of the harbor now; a half-dozen sailors were hoisting the yard and unfurling the sail. Aristarchus, the first mate, was in command of the operation.

Jesus was happy that the rabbi taught them Greek in school at Nazareth, for he was now able to understand the commands Aristarchus was giving and the yells and shouts one sailor hurled at another. He smiled as he recalled how loudly he and his schoolmates complained about those lessons. James protested the loudest; he said he was a Jew and let the rabbi know most vehemently that he only wanted to be a Jew. He wondered what Simon and James and his other friends in Nazareth were doing now. Probably just rising. He wondered, too, if they wondered if they would ever use the Greek shoved so mercilessly down their throats by the stern and strict rabbi.

Suddenly he caught his breath. The sail opened to the wind and the ship was gliding smoothly and rapidly across the water. The sail was beautiful, a work of art in its own right. Jesus estimated that the sail was at least twenty feet wide and fifteen feet high. Its pieces of canvas were sewn together by strips of leather thread. The most beautiful thing about this graceful, wind-filled sail was the magnificent lion painted on both sides in a brilliant golden color. Beneath and above the lion was a row of trumpets, joining together to make a frieze. These were painted in deep, rich red, almost the color of porphyry.

Joseph of Arimathea, thought Jesus, was a man of details. A native of Judea, he carried with him on his travels the symbol of his birthplace, the lion of Judah. A man of deep faith, no wonder Joseph called his ship *Jubilee*. The trumpets on the sails represented the year of jubilee prescribed by the ancients of Israel. Jesus recalled the command in the Torah:

> And on the tenth day of the seventh month you shall sound the trumpet; on the Day of Atonement you shall sound the trumpet throughout the land. You will declare this fiftieth year sacred and proclaim the liberation of all the inhabitants of the land. This is to be a jubilee for you; each of you will return to his ancestral home, each to his own clan.

"God be praised, Jesus! Did you sleep well?" Joseph stood beside him.

"God be praised! I did indeed," said Jesus, for a moment startled by Joseph's presence.

"Your father should be well on his way home by now," Joseph said. "Nicodemus and I will be busy today in the hold, checking the cargo against the inventory. We will have time on the journey to visit. Now I meant to introduce you to the ship's captain, who will assign a task for you."

"I will do anything he asks," Jesus replied.

"Good!" Joseph smiled. "I am sure Alexander has already thought of just the right job for you. He is a man of much experience and great wisdom."

Together they walked toward the stern of the ship where Alexander was standing next to the steering rudders being handled by a young, handsome, muscular sailor. The thumping of the drum had stopped, the thirty sailors who had manned the oars and set the sail in place were resting, enjoying the morning northeastern breeze as it filled the sail and swept across the ship. By now the sun stood high above the hills of Palestine, bathing the shore in a golden brown and distilling the water into a blue deeper than the sky.

"God be with you, Captain Alexander," Joseph greeted him, although he knew the Greek did not even believe in his own gods.

"Good morning to you, sir," the captain replied.

"This, Alexander, is my young friend, Jesus, the son of Joseph the carpenter of Nazareth. I told you he would be traveling with us."

"Pleased to meet you, lad." With the captain, no matter how old or experienced you were, you were always "lad."

"And I, sir, am pleased to meet you." Jesus looked at the rugged, weather-beaten face of the captain, who looked as if he were born to be a man of the sea. The captain's jaw was as square as his shoulders and he looked the type that could face any storm straight in the eye. His body was trim and muscular, and he stood over six feet tall, taller than any man Jesus had ever seen. His feet stood firmly on the deck and Jesus thought they looked as if they had been planted there from the day of his birth. His eyes were clear blue, revealing a sharpness and quickness of mind. The captain allowed himself the distinction of a beard that wrapped itself around his lips and came to a point several inches beneath his chin. This was his distinction, for no other member of the crew was allowed to sport a beard. Everything about the man spoke that he was a born leader and knew well how to exercise his authority. Jesus liked him instinctively and felt, as the captain surveyed him, that the feeling was mutual.

"Now, lad," this tower of a man was saying, "We must get to work. We will have time for talk later. Your duty will be to help the cook in the galley. The cook needs an extra hand and you fill the bill."

"Yes, sir," said Jesus.

"Mate," the captain spoke in a gruffer tone, "take Jesus to Simon in the galley. I'll take the rudder."

"Yes, sir," Aristarchus replied quickly and, turning to Jesus, said, "My name is Aristarchus."

"And my name is Jesus." They clasped hands firmly for a moment, stepped down from the platform and walked toward the galley.

"I watched you come aboard last night," said Aristarchus. "We were expecting you, for Joseph told the captain we would have a young passenger. Most merchant ships carry passengers, you know, but Joseph of Arimathea does not bother with them on his vessel. But I did not think you would be so young."

"I do not think you are much older than I," said Jesus, smiling.

Aristarchus was tall, thin, and quick in all his actions. He spoke Greek, but with an accent that betrayed he was not born Greek. His body was sinewy and his muscles taut. His hair was the color of cottonwood leaves in autumn and curls protruded from the round, brown cap that covered his crown. His eyes were light brown, sparkling with affability and laughter.

"I am twenty," Aristarchus replied. He tested with his hands the fastness of the crates stacked on the deck, forming only a narrow passageway to the galley. "But I have been at sea since I was fourteen, so I know very well the ways of the world. You look like no more than a boy."

This time Jesus smiled. "I am fourteen and among my people that makes me a man. But the farthest I have been from home has been Jerusalem. So you see, my friend, I do not know the ways of your world."

Aristarchus liked his honesty and forthrightness. Perhaps the Jews were not the cunning, shifty people he always thought. At least the two, Joseph and Nicodemus, the only two he knew, were not. He admired and respected Joseph the merchant very much. He felt an immediate liking for this young man who had just now called him friend.

"Here we are," the first mate said and added quickly, "My friends call me Ari."

Jesus looked around. It was not like his mother's kitchen. This was no more than a pile of boxes around a space about six feet square. Above the space an awning was slung from four poles, one in each corner. Goatskins hung haphazardly from the piles and rocked to and fro with the rhythm of the waves. They contained water and wine. In the middle of the square was a circular iron platform with a fire smoldering within and above it hung a huge cast-iron cauldron filled with something that smelled very good to Jesus. It was porridge, seasoned with nutmeg and heavily loaded with raisins, dates, and prunes.

"Simon, meet our passenger, Jesus of Nazareth. The captain has assigned him the task of being your assistant." Ari went fishing for a date in the porridge but caught only a swat from Simon's spoon.

"I'm pleased to meet you, Jesus, and glad the captain has given me a helper. I have been watching you since you came aboard. I am the lucky one. May Yahweh be praised."

"And I am happy to be assigned to work with you, Simon." Jesus was surprised to hear him invoke God's holy name. He wondered if Simon was a Jew. Time would tell.

"Now to work," said Simon as Ari disappeared. "Before meals, Jesus, your job will be to set out the bowls, spoons, and mugs on the counter--those boxes over there serve as the counter. You must set out, let's see, thirty-four--no, thirty-five. That includes the sailors, the first-mate, the captain, Joseph, Nicodemus, you and me. I guess that makes thirty-six." He smiled.

"Do we all eat together?"

"By all means," exclaimed Simon. Again he smiled and added, "Joseph insists that on his ship all receive the same food. And I try to make it the best I can. It also saves a lot of time."

"Do they eat this way on all merchant ships?"

"Oh, no," exclaimed Simon. "But Joseph is a very good man, even though the crew doesn't always respond. He tries to treat everyone as a brother and hopes that all will act as brothers."

"Simon, are you a Jew? Like Joseph?"

"No, but we can talk about that later. Let's get to work now. And as soon as the crew is finished you can start washing the bowls and mugs and spoons. Might as well get used to it, Jesus, for that's what you'll be doing the entire voyage, every morning and evening."

Jesus went to work.

The ship's bell clanged and the crew surrounded the galley from every corner of the deck. Jesus emerged from the hold in the company of some sailors. He noticed the captain had turned the rudder over to Ari, stepped down from the platform, and strode toward the galley. Sailors deferred to him as he passed.

For the first time Jesus noticed the aft-sail billowing in the wind above the Ari's head. It was also a work of art. Although only one-quarter the size of the main sail, it was painted a brilliant scarlet and emblazoned in the center was a golden menorah. Jesus was proud that Joseph was not ashamed to let the whole Mediterranean world know his Jewish ancestry.

Joseph now stood beside the captain. The sailors, many of whom had shipped out on other voyages with Joseph, stood around the galley waiting for Joseph to begin. Joseph bowed his head for the blessing he invoked before every meal on the journey:

> Bless Yahweh, my soul,
> Yahweh my God, how great you are!
> Clothed in majesty and glory,
> wrapped in a robe of light!
> ...you make fresh grass grow for cattle
> and those plants made use of by man,
> for them to get food from the soil;
> wine to make them cheerful,
> oil to make them happy
> and bread to make them strong.

As Joseph prayed, the captain stood in respect, a few sailors bowed their heads but most cast fidgety glances at the sails, the sea, and the shoreline. The sun had edged its way to the center of the sky.

Joseph finished and the deck rocked with chatter and laughter and good-natured jostling for position in line. Captain Alexander led the line, followed by Joseph, Nicodemus, and the crew. As each passed, Simon poured out a helping of porridge in each bowl and as each man passed he reached into a barrel for a hard roll. Jesus' task was to keep their mugs filled with wine. Some of the crew greeted him as he passed; others looked at him and recognized him as Joseph's young friend. Simon and Jesus helped themselves when all the others had been served.

"It might not be what Augustus has in his palace," Simon said, pointing to a packing crate next to him for Jesus to sit on, "but it's good, solid food. Kind a sailor needs." They ate in silence, and Jesus noticed most of the crew did also.

"When you are finished with your chores, Jesus, come back and we can talk." The captain was walking past him, not even pausing to stop or so much as look at him. Others were close behind him, setting their utensils back on the counter. On ship a meal was not a social event.

Simon rose and Jesus followed him. The water was heated in the cauldron over the big, black fire-box, waiting for the utensils to be washed. Jesus set to his task as Simon busied himself with his own work. Jesus knew as did all the crew that this was Simon's kingdom.

"You are a lucky young man, Jesus," Simon was half talking and half thinking to himself, "to have such a friend as Joseph to take you along on this journey. I often wished my sons could have sailed with me when they were younger."

Jesus turned and looked at Simon for a moment. He saw a man who looked no more than thirty, rather tall, with rough, angular facial features. He noticed his hands; they were large and strong, capable of carrying crates and jars of great weight.

"You are married then, Simon?"

"Yes, and happy too. My wife, Esther, is as beautiful as they say your Queen Esther was. I have two daughers and two sons, but the boys are no longer at home."

"Where are they?"

"In Rome. You will meet them there."

"They must be very young," said Jesus.

"Not so, unless you call yourself young. One is about your age and the other, let's see, is sixteen."

"And your daughters?" Jesus did not want to seem inquisitive but he was genuinely interested in everything about Simon.

"Oh, they are still children, at home with their mother. Rebecca is six, I think, and Leah is eleven."

"I must go now, Simon, to see the captain."

"Good," Simon replied. "It is time for my nap."

As Jesus walked toward the captain's deck he noticed something else about the ship he did not see before. The railings around the deck were painted scarlet and blue, red and gold to match the colors on the sails. The railings came together at the stern, their colors blending into a sunset golden hue at the gooseneck. Fastened to the end of the gooseneck was a brass triangle. He could not figure that out; someday he would ask Joseph.

"There you are, lad," the captain said. "We have a fair wind today so it is smooth sailing. Aristarchus, we call him Ari, went to stretch out on his mat. Before I do and turn the rudder back to him I thought I would see how you are doing. You're not seasick?"

"No, sir."

"You like Simon?"

"Yes, sir."

"He's a good cook. This is his ninth or tenth time out with me, but not always on the *Jubilee*. Do you like Joseph's ship?"

"Very much, sir. It is a beautiful ship. I have never before seen anything like it."

"Suppose not. Suppose all you have ever seen were those miserable little boats the fishermen of Capernaum call ships. And they call that little pond a lake! Ha! Those poor Galileans! They would not know what to do with a ship if you gave them one as a gift. Due apologies to you, lad."

"Those boats on the Sea of Galilee were all that I had ever seen before yesterday," Jesus replied. "My people do not know much about the sea and its distance and depth, sir. I suppose that is why they fear it."

"But why are you making this journey?"

"Joseph of Arimathea invited me," Jesus replied. "And I also have my own special reason."

"And what might that be, lad?"

"I cannot tell you that now, Captain. Maybe later."

"Oh! That very special reason must be terribly important!" Jesus felt the teasing in the captain's voice.

"It is." Jesus' voice was firm and the captain felt the seriousness in the reply of the young man who sounded more serious than one would expect from a youth his age.

Alexander said nothing for several minutes. The waves gently lapped against the ship as it rocked rhythmically forward over the water. Jesus recalled the warmth he felt as his mother used to cradle him in her arms and here, sitting beside Alexander, he felt as secure as he did long ago in Nazareth.

"We will have to talk more about that later, Jesus. You had better go below. Joseph may be wondering what you are doing."

Jesus rose and as he left he noticed the captain was gazing pensively across the waters. The Greek was thinking.

* * * * * *

"There you are!" exclaimed Joseph as Jesus stood at the foot of the stairs in the hold. "Nicodemus and I have just been talking about you."

"I was with the captain, Joseph."

Jesus glanced about the hold and noticed row after row of packing crates and between them rows of large earthen jars called amphorae. He also noticed he was standing on a pile of wheat; the whole floor of the hold was covered with wheat. He stooped down and gathered a handful of it.

"That," said Joseph as he walked toward him, "is from Galilee. I bought it from a merchant in Sophoris and it was raised on the Plain of Esdralon. We use it as ballast for the ship, but when we arrive in Puteoli I will sell it at a good price. The Romans are always demanding wheat. Even this little bit will bring a good price."

Nicodemus emerged from one of the caverns of packing crates and came toward them. "You have come down now, Jesus," he said jokingly, "just when we finished the inventory. But you have your own job."

"Simon was pleased," Jesus replied. "Could you tell me what is in all those boxes and huge pots?" Jesus noted that Nicodemus had three large scrolls tucked under his arm and presumed they contained an inventory.

"Come," said Joseph, leading the way, "let us go topside. There Nick, that's what we call him for short, can tell you what cargo we have and I can give my account to Captain Alexander." Nick motioned Jesus to follow Joseph and in a few moments the threesome stood by the railing.

Joseph looked at the sun in the west and walked over to the deck beneath the captain's platform. He turned and said, "Jesus, you had better wait until after dinner to talk with Nick. I am sure Simon will be looking for you."

As a matter of fact, Simon was already stirring about his little kingdom. Jesus greeted him, "Blessed be our great

Yahweh!" He noticed Simon liked the greeting and smiled. Jesus went to the boxes and began setting out the bowls and mugs.

"Tonight, my young man, we will have fresh fruit. Peaches and pears and figs from your country. You can dig out those wooden bowls there and put the fruit in them."

"What are you cooking in the kettle, Simon? It smells good."

"Mutton stew, fresh mutton stew, with carrots, peas, onions, and just enough garlic to make many of these men think of home." As good cooks everywhere, Simon was proud of his menu.

"Where are most of the sailors from, Simon?" Jesus hoped he did not offend Simon by being more interested in the men than the menu.

"Oh, from Dalmatia, from Thessaly, most of them. The others from other parts of Greece," Simon answered as he continued cutting carrots into the stew. "They make good seamen, says the captain. And I say they should because their ancestors for generations were among the best pirates that ever sailed these waters. The Dalmatians, especially, centuries ago raided most of the cities along the coast, like my own Cyrene."

"They were pirates?"

"Not the kind of brigands you know, son, along the highways in your country. They were robbers, not cutthroats. In fact, when the great-grandfathers of these men roved these waters, piracy was considered as honorable a trade as being a merchant or longshoreman. Today the men from these countries are considered the best among all sailors."

Jesus thought a few moments as he continued setting out the utensils. "But Ari told me he was from Macedonia."

"He is, and about five of the new sailors he brought along with him are from Thessalonica. They are also good sailors, almost as good as their ancestors who conquered the world under their great King Alexander."

"Are they also Greeks?" Jesus asked.

"Greeks? Of course. You might say as some do that the Macedonians under Alexander made Greece the great power it was. Talk to the captain about that. He likes to brag about his country."

After dinner Jesus did his chores, becoming more familiar with all the cabinets and shelves in the galley. Simon finished his duties and went off to write a letter to his wife and daughters.

Jesus stood amidship by the railing, studying the tiny lights that began shining on the distant shore. He liked the ship very much and was beginning to understand how easily sailors become attached to their vessels. He noticed Captain Alexander was again manning the rudder and felt safe from all harm. And he wondered where they were and what route they would be taking to Rome. Joseph and Nick were walking toward him. He noticed that Nick had a scroll tucked under his arm.

"Now we have time, Jesus, to tell you what cargo is below." Nick began unrolling the scroll as he stood beside Jesus. "We have been fortunate in the loading of the ship. We have suffered no breakage, only one cracked amphora, and the side of one crate has come loose. Your cedar chests are packed neatly and firmly between the crates."

"Nick," said Joseph hurriedly, "read from your list so that Jesus knows what merchandise we will deliver to our agent in Rome."

Nick stretched out his hands, one firmly on each end of the papyrus sheet, and read: "Twenty jars of Judean wine, five jars of frankincense, ten jars of black pepper, fifty rolls of finished papyrus, thirty jars of smoked fish, ten bolts of fine Egyptian linen, four tons of copper, and eight tons of tin."

"And there will be more when we dock at Seleucia." Nick was rolling up the scroll as Joseph made that remark.

"Isn't that an awful lot already?" asked Jesus.

"Not for the *Jubilee*," said Joseph. "She is capable of carrying fifty tons. We have now about thirty tons and will pick up about another twenty tomorrow in Seleucia. There you will see some of the bigger Roman ships. Especially those of the emperor's own fleet that transport grain from Egypt. Some of those ships hold over a thousand tons."

"What kind of cargo will we be picking up tomorrow in that strange-sounding name of a port?" Jesus' face revealed his wonderment.

"Seleucia," Joseph answered, "is a Greek city, one of the busiest ports in the Mediterranean. It is the gateway to the vast countries of Persia, India, and even Cathay. For that reason I have an office in Seleucia and a man there who serves as my purchasing agent. His name is Barnabas. He really lives in Antioch but maintains the office in Seleucia. Antioch is a Syrian city, you know, and Barnabas is a Jew like us."

"In Seleucia," Nick added, "Barnabas should have for us about a hundred bolts of silk from Damascus and about five hundred jars of Syrian wine. For some reason I cannot understand, the Romans have cultivated a taste for the wines of Syria. I suspect it is just because they are more expensive."

They had not noticed that the sun had dipped beneath the western rim and dusk had settled over them. Nicodemus excused himself and went off to attend to some minor details with Aristarchus.

"Have you enjoyed the day, Jesus?" Joseph now realized

this was the first chance he had to talk to his young friend alone.

"Very much, Joseph. It has all been a wonderment to me. I do not know how I will ever repay you for taking me along."

"Some day you might," Joseph said. "We never really know what the future holds."

"That's true, Joseph, and I am certain that some day I will repay you."

Joseph was struck by the remark and wondered if it were the words or the gravity of his friend that caused his wonder. Darkness had fallen and here and there lights were twinkling along the shoreline, matching, but not excelling, the brilliance of the stars. The movement of the ship over the water and the gentle lapping of the waves against its sides were soothing and relaxing. On other parts of the deck sailors had gathered in small groups, softly talking and occasionally piercing the silence with a shrill whistle or loud laughter. They were talking of home, their girl friends and the good times they expected on shore leave. Near the stern a group was shooting dice. Joseph carelessly wondered how many drachmas would change hands that night.

"Joseph," said Jesus, interrupting his thoughts, "may I ask you a personal question?"

"By all means."

"It seems strange to me," Jesus continued, "that you should be an international merchant. I always thought that our people were farmers or shepherds or small shopkeepers. What ever moved you to choose this business?"

"In a word, Jesus, money!" Joseph laughed out loud.

Jesus looked disappointed and puzzled. "There must be more," he said thoughtfully.

"And there is, Jesus. My father was a merchant and I followed in his steps just as you now follow in your father's steps as a carpenter. I expanded the enterprise by purchasing the *Jubilee*, because, to me, money represents power, and I pray to Yahweh that I might some day have power to help our people from the oppression they suffer. Some day, too, I hope to be a member of our Sanhedrin, and in that way possibly be of even greater help to our people."

"Does your wife share this desire with you?" Jesus knew he was prying but he felt that Joseph did not mind.

"Of course she does, Jesus. She is a kind, good, loving woman. She is always taking the sick and homeless into our home in Arimathea. Some day I hope to teach my oldest son, Josephes, to do the same. He is a fine boy, Jesus, eight years old now. I hope that he will turn out to be a young man like you."

"Thank you, Joseph."

"But there is more, Jesus, to all this shipping and bargaining than just that. I know you have read our prophets and I think you know them better than I. But there is one passage in the writings of Zechariah that I think of often. You recall he wrote, 'Many peoples and great nations will come to seek Yahweh Sabaoth in Jerusalem and to entreat the favor of Yahweh.'"

"I remember, too," Jesus replied, "that Zechariah also wrote, 'Rejoice heart and soul, daughter of Zion! Shout with gladness, daughter of Jerusalem! So now, your king comes to you; he is victorious, he is triumphant, humble and riding on a donkey, on a colt, the foal of a donkey.'"

"And that, Jesus, was the reason Zechariah was so busy with rebuilding the temple. And that is why through all this trading and traveling, I hope in some way to make the name of our great God better known among these Greeks and Romans." Joseph paused and gazed across the water.

"Did you ever think," Jesus spoke softly after a few moments, "that you might build temples to Yahweh in Greece and Rome and even beyond, like in the Spain and Britain these sailors talk about? Perhaps, Joseph, our God can be worshiped any place and not just in Jerusalem."

Joseph pondered these words. No wonder the doctors and the teachers in Jerusalem marveled at this young man when he spoke with them in the temple several years ago. These words were strange, indeed, for Jewish ears. It was best to say no more.

"It is time, Jesus," Joseph spoke with affection, "to go to bed. The morning will come soon enough and we will be busy in Seleucia. Good night, Jesus. God be with you."

"Good night, Joseph. God also be with you."

Joseph stood by the railing, looking at the stars, then the coastline, then about the ship now wrapped in sleep and silence.

Jesus stood by his mat, also gazing at the stars all around him and he thought in their own way they were praising Yahweh by their brightness. He studied that lesser orb called the moon, casting shadows in the darkness by its fullness and serving God's creatures as a lesser light in the darkness. Jesus lifted his head to Yahweh and in his heart uttered the prayer he was taught long ago by his mother in Nazareth:

> Praise God in his temple on earth,
> > praise him in his temple in heaven,
> > praise him for his mighty achievements,
> > praise him for his transcendent greatness!
> Praise him with blasts of the trumpet,
> > praise him with lyre and harp,
> > praise him with drums and dancing,
> > praise him with strings and reeds,
> > praise him with clashing cymbals,

praise him with clanging cymbals!
Let everything that breathes praise Yahweh!

* * * * * *

The next day the *Jubilee* sailed into the port of Seleucia, carefully treading its way through a forest of masts and sails. The noise, the feverish hustling of the people on ships and docks, the yelling and shouting and cursing of the gods made Jerusalem during the Passover seem like a quiet family gathering in Nazareth. Never had Jesus seen anything like this. Never had he seen so many different kinds of people, all kinds of clothing, some clad in bright and rich robes and others with no more than a loin cloth tied about their waists. He could not count the camels and donkeys and mules that moved back and forth along the streets leading down to the docks. Stevedores no more than a notch above slaves rubbed shoulders with wealthy and powerful merchants and dealers from Antioch, Damascus, and distant India.

"Good morning, Jesus." Nick was by his side.

"Good morning, Nick. Shalom!"

Nick had forgotten the traditional greeting of his people. "I see you are amazed," he went on, "by all this activity. It is a much bigger port than Caesarea."

"I am," said Jesus. "I have never seen so many different kinds of people. Who are they?"

"Some are Phoenician and Syrian sailors, some are Armenian slaves owned by wealthy and retired Romans who control this port, others are traders from Cappadocia, Galacia, and those dark brown people are from far away India. Those who are richly dressed and wear jewels around their necks and on their fingers are mostly silk merchants from

Damascus. They like to make a show of their wealth."

"Do they know our great God?"

"Some may have heard about him in their travels and there may even be a few who are God-fearing, but most of them still worship their own gods and carry little statues of them around with them. Of course, most of the Greeks and Romans scoff at their own gods. They call the stories about them nothing but fables, which they are."

"I feel sad that they do not know our God. They must be very lonely people," said Jesus. "Nick, they have never heard the words of our Law: 'Yahweh your God you shall follow, him you shall fear, his commandments you shall keep, his voice you shall obey, him shall you serve, to him shall you cling.' They have no one to cling to!"

"I know. I know. That is why I have chosen to join Joseph in this business. Some people say the business of business is to make money. I think, like Joseph, that our business is also to make the name of Yahweh known among all these people."

"I think you will, Nick, and I think you will be very good at it."

Nick passed over that remark. He had a message for Jesus and had almost forgotten it.

"Jesus, Joseph asked me to tell you to remain on board. We will be here only long enough to pick up our cargo and set sail again. I think Joseph is afraid you might get lost among the crowds on the dock. He told me how you once got lost in Jerusalem a few years ago and how upset your parents were. I suppose he does not want that to happen again."

"I will stay on the ship," Jesus replied. "I want to talk to Ari and ask him some questions anyway."

"When Barnabas, our agent, comes aboard I want you to meet him. You will like him. Everyone does."

Nick turned and descended the gangplank. A few minutes later Jesus watched him with his scrolls tucked under his right arm mingling about the crowd on the dock, talking briefly, now to one and then another. Jesus looked down the side of the ship and noticed that stevedores were already carrying in huge jars of Syrian wine. Another line of slaves seemed to him like an endless procession carrying bolts of Damascus silk. Joseph and Captain Alexander wanted to spend as little time as possible in Seleucia; neither liked the officials there nor the motley mass of men milling about its docks and warehouses.

Jesus continued to wonder how many men and women in years to come would sail from this port, carrying the name of the great Yahweh to the Greeks and Romans as Joseph and Nicodemus were intent upon doing today. He glanced back at the platform and saw Aristarchus relaxing beside the motionless rudder. He did not seem busy so Jesus walked over to him.

"Good morning, Ari. Shalom!"

"And good morning to you, my friend. And what does that 'shalom' mean?"

"It means, 'Peace be with you!' I mean it from my heart."

"You will discover, if you haven't already, that the only peace we have comes to us because of the Roman army."

"On the contrary, Ari," Jesus replied. "I believe that peace comes to us from our great Yahweh. We can have peace without any armies."

"Well, let's agree to disagree on that." Aristarchus flashed a smile.

"Now, if you are not too busy, I have some questions to ask."

"I am not busy, just watching the crowd down there on the dock. Come up here and sit down." Jesus stepped up and seated himself on the floor of the platform. "Now, what's on your mind?"

"I am curious about our journey, Ari."

Aristarchus liked the smile that crossed the young man's face. Jesus, he thought, was really not that much younger than himself and perhaps in time they could be good friends.

"They say curiosity killed the cat. I'm sure it won't kill you, Jesus." Ari smiled again.

"I would like to know what route we will be taking to Rome. It seems strange to me that so far we have been sailing northeast, and Rome, I thought, was west of Caesarea."

"You are right," said Ari. "But there is a good reason for that, and only sailors would know it. You see, the prevailing winds in the Mediterranean are northeasterly, and they sometimes blow down from the north with the ferocity of a tiger. For that reason Captain Alexander, like all seaworthy captains, including those who run the clipper fleet of grain from Egypt, hug the shoreline and set the sail against the winds. It is not safe to sail directly across the sea."

"That makes sense," said Jesus.

"Those same winds," Ari continued, "limit our sailing season between spring and autumn. They bring clouds over the blue waters, making them gray during the winter months. When the navigator cannot see the sun during the day or the stars at night, he does not know what direction the ship is taking. For that reason many ships that sail during winter are lost or wrecked on rocky shores."

"I have heard the fishermen on the Sea of Galilee sometimes call you 'summer sailors,' " Jesus said.

"That is only because they don't know the limitations of navigation and the treachery of these waters. It is not fear, Jesus, but good common sense."

"You called the ships that carry grain from Egypt a fleet.

When I was very small, I lived in Egypt for some time, about two years, as an exile. That was the time when King Herod killed all the baby boys in Bethlehem. Why, Ari, do they call these ships a fleet?"

"Because there are hundreds of them, Jesus. They are good, solid ships, serving as a passenger line as much as a source of supply. When we come to Rome, you will see how immense a city it is, and all those people have to be fed. Over two hundred thousand of these Romans are on the emperor's dole. The mighty Augustus soon realized that to keep his throne he had to keep these people fed and entertained. So he built this fleet and made it a function of the state. For all practical purposes, it is part of the Roman navy. Augustus learned his lesson at the battle of Actium some fifty years ago that whoever controlled the Mediterranean was master of the empire. In a few short years he built a navy out of almost nothing. Of course, Agrippa did it, but Augustus got the credit. People call him the father of the Roman navy."

"The emperor must be a very great man," said Jesus. "I hope to meet him."

"Ha! You do not meet the emperor; he meets you, and only if he wants to. He is a very private man, they say, and does not like to be seen in public more than he must. No Jesus, we will not see him, and you will not meet him."

Jesus thought quietly for several moments, gazing about at the whirl of activity all around the ship. Ari called to a sailor to bring a flask of wine and two mugs. He reached into the cabinet of the bench on which he was sitting and pulled out a large, well-worn parchment.

"Now," he said, "here is the map of this ocean. I can show you on here better than I can explain where the captain will be steering the *Jubilee* in the coming weeks." He unfolded the parchment across his sitting bench and set the two mugs the sailor had brought at each end and the bottle of wine in the middle. Jesus rose and crouched down beside him.

"Here we are today," Ari said, pointing his finger at the spot marked "Seleucia." It was at the far eastern end of the Mediterranean Sea above a country marked "Phoenecia." He moved his finger along the coastline of a country called "Cilicia" and then continued. "In a few days we should be at Tarsus to take on water and fresh supplies. I don't like Tarsus. It is a Roman colony with a Roman procurator and a university. The citizens there like to let everyone know they are citizens of Rome. They think they are better than us Greeks and they try to show it. Mostly retired Roman army officers and soldiers."

"But, Ari," Jesus interrupted, "you know there is really no difference between Greeks and Romans and anyone else in the sight of Yahweh! Some day perhaps somebody from Tarsus might get that idea and spread it to all the Greeks and Romans."

Ari ignored the remark. "Anyway, I am glad we will dock there only a few hours. Then we will sail along this coastline here beneath this land marked 'Pamphylia' and in about six or seven days we will come to Myra. We dock there and spend an overnight so that everyone will have leave."

"Simon told me," said Jesus, "there is a synagogue of my people in Myra. Are there any God-fearing Greeks in Myra?"

"I do not know what you mean by that, Jesus."

"I mean, are there any Greeks who are friends of our synagogue and believe in Yahweh the one true God?"

"I don't know a thing about that, Jesus. You see, I know nothing about your God and do not believe in our Greek gods so I just don't know. I think Urban, Joseph's agent in

Rome, is one of those kind of people you talk about. Anyway," and Ari took a gulp of wine and went back to his finger on the map.

"From Myra we will sail along the coast of Lycia—see here!—passing above the island of Rhodes and after about five days anchor at Cnidus. We won't stop long, though, just time enough to take on fresh water and supplies. We then hurry on to Salmone on the island of Crete, stop for supples, sail under the belly of Crete to protect us from the northeastern winds and then stop either at Lasea or Phoenix, depending on how badly we need supplies." Ari took another swallow of wine and so did Jesus.

"Have you met Barnabas yet?"

"No, but Nick said he will come aboard when finished with his business. Why do you ask?"

"Because Barnabas always says he would like to live on the island of Crete. Everybody likes Barnabas."

"I'm anxious to meet him."

"So on we go," Ari continued. "The next part of our journey will be the most dangerous. It will be the longest stretch of open sea we will cross and there old Neptune likes to destroy ships and sailors when he is angry. At least that is what they say. But it is really the ferocious gusts of winds that come ripping out of the north. It takes a good captain, Jesus, to make it through this stretch."

"Captain Alexander is a good captain!"

"One of the best. He had made this journey many times, and with his skill, and a little luck, always made it through."

Ari was again pointing at the map. "After about another dozen days, we will reach Syracuse on this island of 'Sicilia.' You will like Syracuse, Jesus, because it is an ancient Greek colony, and the people there are just like us Greeks."

Jesus smiled. "I wonder, Ari, if you sometimes forget

that there are other people in the world just as good and great as the Greeks. I happen to think that my people are God's chosen race, but I also know that other people—we call them Gentiles—are also good and great people."

"I know, I know, but sometimes I forget." Ari was impatient now, more with his own narrowness than with Jesus' remark. "At any rate, we will take on fresh supplies in Syracuse and if the captain thinks we have enough time, he will give all on board an overnight leave. The next day we head for Rhegium, take on supplies, pass through the Strait of Messina, which is sometimes a very treacherous passage, depending on the winds. If we clear that passage, the rest of the journey is a cinch. In four or five days we will be sailing into Puteoli, which, you know, is a port of Rome."

"And how long will the journey take?"

"Fifty days if we are lucky, perhaps sixty."

"Thank you, Ari. Now I have some idea where we are going."

"No trouble, Jesus." Ari emptied his mug and started folding the chart. "I enjoyed showing you how we will get to Puteoli."

Just then shouts and yells and laughter pierced the calmness on the deck. A booming voice was yelling above all the noise on the pier.

"Where's the boy? Where's this young friend of Joseph? He said I must meet him!"

"That," said Ari, "is Barnabas. You always hear him before you see him. He is a Jew like you, and don't tell me Greeks brag too much because he brags about his people more than ten of us do." Jesus watched a small, short, wisp-of-a-man come almost rolling over the railing. Could such a thunderous voice emerge from such a tiny body! Barnabas was coming toward him, almost running like a little rooster in a garden. Joseph's agent had a long, thin face and hands that matched. His pitch-black beard accentuated the blackness of his deep-set eyes. If his actions were not so lively and his gait so brisk, one would think he was undernourished.

"Ahhh! There you are! The carpenter of Nazareth whom Joseph is trying to make a merchant!" Barnabas was beside him, yet his voice was still booming. He did not wait for a reply. "I told Joseph he should leave you here with me in Seleucia and I would make you my apprentice. How would you like that? Well, he's the boss and said you go with him. Perhaps next time?"

"I am Joseph's guest, you know," Jesus replied.

Barnabas barely heard the reply for immediately he went on. "May Yahweh forgive me! Jesus, I forgot to greet you. May the God of Abraham, Isaac, and Jacob bless you; may his countenance shine upon you. Shalom!"

"Shalom! Barnabas." Jesus bowed slightly and smiled.

"You are, as Joseph said, a fine young man, Jesus. I hope these Greeks like Ari here will not corrupt you!" He roared another loud laugh. "Of course, I am only kidding, you know. Captain Alexander would be lost without you, Ari, and he knows it, but you better not let him know that you know it."

"Barnabas," Jesus said, "when Ari was showing me the route of our journey, he told me that you like Crete very much." Jesus was leading the conversation away from Ari, for he knew his friend was embarrassed by Barnabas's good-natured remark.

"Indeed I do, young man, indeed I do. If the great Yahweh wills it, I should like very much some day to retire there with my wife and with my children like potted plants all around us."

"You are too young to think about retiring," Ari interrupted. "You have many years of work ahead of you, scheming and bargaining with these Syrians and Indians."

"But a person has to plan ahead," said Barnabas. "You know the saying, 'a stitch in time saves nine.' Oh, I guess that doesn't apply, does it? Anyway, you know what I mean."

"And I was taught in school at Nazareth," Jesus interrupted, "that Yahweh said, 'My thoughts are not your thoughts and my ways are not your ways.'"

"Now," cried Barnabas, "you both have me in a corner! Two against one is not fair."

"What would you say, Barnabas, if you retired in Cyprus instead of Crete?" Jesus asked the question with a seriousness and steadiness that even disarmed Barnabas for a moment.

"No, I still would take Crete."

"Time will tell," said Jesus.

"Shalom!" Barnabas shouted as if he were standing on the dock below. He scampered across the deck and hurried to the gangplank. He turned back to the two and shouted, "If I have to say so myself, I struck some very good bargains for Joseph this time." He disappeared over the side of the ship.

Ari looked at Jesus and both smiled. "I don't know," said Ari, "if he was talking to us or to himself about his business ability. I do know, though, that Joseph values him very highly."

Jesus thanked Ari again and said it was time to help Simon with the meal. Ari told him to tell Simon to be generous with the helpings for the crew would be very hungry.

Jesus walked toward the galley, wondering about the long journey ahead for the *Jubilee*.

4

The Beautiful Blue Sea

The next morning the *Jubilee* was gliding smoothly over the water again, the wind filling her sails and her crew enjoying the warmth of a sunny spring morning. The ship followed the coastline, as Ari had said. The crew was relaxed and in good humor. Simon told Jesus that the crew Captain Alexander picked was always a little above average and were usually content because they respected the captain. They also knew that Joseph of Arimathea was an honorable man and he always treated them with dignity and respect. Some members of the crew even said he was that way because of the worship of his one God whom they knew he called Yahweh.

Day followed day in a regular routine which was far from monotonous for Jesus. He took in every sight, every sound, alert to the change in winds, the smell of the sea, the clucking of sea gulls that followed the ship and the hearty shouts of both crews as the *Jubilee* passed other ships.

The overnight stop in Myra afforded Jesus the opportunity to visit a city made beautiful by Grecian art and architecture. Nick was his guide and together they returned to the ship at nightfall. They had briefly visited the synagogue in Myra and greeted the rabbi. He was friendly and surprised to meet a young man from little-known Galilee on such a journey.

The days passed swiftly. They passed under the belly of Crete, all one hundred sixty miles of it, said Simon. One morning Jesus noticed they had left the shoreline. He figured the ship was now out in the deep waters of the treacherous part of the trip that Ari explained. Here Captain Alexander showed his great skill as a seaman.

The merchant of Arimathea, however, was relaxed. He had the greatest confidence in the mastery of Alexander. Also, his cargo was complete and the hold was full, or nearly so. "We have only a small space left," he said to Jesus one evening as they were sitting on the deck. "We still may fill it with some wheat in Syracuse. The Romans never seem to have enough grain."

"How long will we be in Rome, Joseph?"

"A week, maybe ten days. We have to wait until the cargo is unloaded at Puteoli and transported to Rome. Of course, we will go on ahead, leaving Nick to supervise the business in Puteoli. In Rome we will take our lodging in the home of Urban, who is my agent."

"We will be busy in Rome, then?"

"I will be busy, Jesus." Joseph laughed heartily. "Urban

and I will be haggling over prices with the merchants. We will be contacting other merchants for orders for next year's shipment. We will have to waste a great deal of time with tax collectors and no doubt, as usual, end up bribing most of them, for that is the way the Romans do business. But you will have time to walk about the largest city in the world and see sights that you have never seen nor ever dreamed."

"Perhaps, then," Jesus said excitedly, "I will see the emperor."

"No, Jesus," said Joseph. "I do not think you will see the emperor. I have been to Rome nine times, even during their festivals, but have never seen him."

"Time will tell," said Jesus, more to himself than Joseph. "But I am eager to see the sights of Rome," he added.

"And you will, but not alone. Ari or Simon, or someone from Urban's office must be with you at all times. If you can get lost in Jerusalem, you will surely get lost in Rome!"

"Will we dock in Syracuse overnight, Joseph?" Jesus hoped the shift in conversation was not too obvious.

"No longer than we have to," Joseph replied, obviously not noticing the sudden shift. "We will take on fresh provisions and see if a grain dealer is on the dock selling grain. It is too bad, too, for you would like Syracuse, Jesus. It is one of the oldest colonies the Greeks founded. Its citizens are strong and vigorous and highly cultured. Somehow they have preserved the best of Grecian art and learning."

"And they have their own gods too?"

"Yes, Jesus. I think every Greek city and village and almost every family has their own gods. I feel sad when I think that they do not know Yahweh."

"Do you think, Joseph, that they will ever come to know and worship Yahweh?"

"I don't know. I don't know. They may come to know him and they may even become devout God-fearing pagans like Simon there." He motioned to Simon puttering among his pots and pans in the galley. "But I do not think they will ever come to worship him as we do. After all, we are his chosen people. Only with our ancestors, Abraham, Isaac, and Jacob, did he make a covenant."

"But don't you think Yahweh could reveal himself to all these good pagan people in other ways than he revealed himself to our fathers?"

"Oh now! That is possible! You know everything is possible with Yahweh, even those things that seem impossible for us."

They sat together in silence. Joseph was watching the sailors, some engaged in what seemed a continuous game of dice and others sitting on packing crates, spinning yarns that in time would become legends and, perhaps, someday, touched by the genius of a poet, become national epics.

Jesus sat gazing at the sun showing only half its orb on the western horizon. He thought of the pagans he had met and seen on this journey, of the sailors he had come to know and like, of the vast number of pagans whom he would never see as far west as Spain and even in that mysterious island called Brittania, about which the sailors told preposterous stories. "What thoughts, my friend are now dancing on the floor of your mind?" Joseph brought Jesus back to the deck of the *Jubilee*.

"I know it may sound strange to you, Joseph, but I was thinking of pagans who do not know Yahweh and who live in that strange-sounding Brittania and whether you will ever go there." Jesus spoke rapidly, the words tumbling over each other as they passed his lips.

Joseph rose and started pacing the deck. "For the carpenter's son of Nazareth, Jesus, you have some very strange and distant ideas! Well, we do not know much about Brittania. We know the mighty Caesar went there, took one look at the fierce natives, put an officer in charge and rushed back to the comparative security of Gaul."

Days passed. Captain Alexander successfully guided the ship through the stormy open sea. Jesus and even some of the sailors were seasick. Within a few days the ship would be anchored in the magnificent harbor of Syracuse.

One night Ari lay on his mat, resting from his day's work. He was tired but not sleepy. He wondered what new events were taking place in his native Thessalonica, what his parents, brothers, and sisters were doing, how well his father's business as a silversmith was going, whether he made a wise choice in taking to the sea and not staying home to work with his father. Most of all he wondered about Elaina.

His heart skipped more than a beat whenever he thought of her. That happened several times every day of the voyage. Would she wait for him? What was she doing now? Home weaving beside her mother? When would he ever have enough money saved to have a home of his own and make her his bride? Could other young men who were more wealthy be calling on her, courting her, wooing her? He prayed to the gods of his city to protect his family, to take him home safely and, most of all, to keep Elaina faithful to him. He startled himself to find that he was praying!

He looked about the deck. Most of his mates were sleeping, some snoring loudly enough to wake all the fish in the sea. He smiled when he glanced at his friend, Sylvanus, the boatswain, who talked in his sleep and unknowingly revealed the secrets of his heart. But Sylvanus was a cheerful man and took the joshings of his mates with good humor. As he turned to the prow, he noticed Jesus silently standing by the railing and gazing at the stars. He wondered what he was thinking. Probably, like himself, of his home, his friends, and his family. Perhaps he was lonesome.

Ari gathered his limbs together and sauntered toward Jesus. "They say there is a man in the moon," Ari spoke softly as he approached Jesus. "But every sailor knows if you look long enough, you can see the face of the woman in the moon."

"Good evening, Ari, or is it morning?" Jesus seemed to welcome his company, for Ari felt his friendship by the smile Jesus gave him. "I was thinking of Yahweh who holds the moon in place century after century as it moves back and forth across our earth."

"There is where you are wrong, Jesus, because you do not know the ways of the sea and the knowledge of the sailors. The moon is a planet, though smaller, just like our earth, and both the moon and the earth revolve around the sun."

"But I thought the earth was flat, like a table, and stood as solidly as my father's workbench in Nazareth."

"So you thought and no doubt were taught, just as millions of other people." Ari chuckled to himself and smiled at his young friend. "But, Jesus, for centuries Greek sailors and navigators have known that the earth is round, not flat. They also knew that if you sail west long enough and far enough, you ultimately go east and return where you started."

"That is amazing," Jesus wondered out loud. "I did not know that men knew that and believed it."

"We have known that for centuries, Jesus. Over a thousand years ago one of our greatest Greek sailors by the name of Jason set sail eastward in a ship rowed by fifty men in search of gold. He sailed into what then was called 'the friendly sea,' which today we call the Black Sea. He explored that sea and had to struggle against icebergs, something no one in our world ever knew of before. He did not find the gold he was seeking but did find a land that was rich in wheat. You know Greece desperately needs wheat because of our rocky land. So Jason was our first exploring sea captain who knew from his voyage that the earth was round. That is why our poets loudly sing his praises in our nation's songs."

"Your Jason must have been a fearless man," Jesus said, for he was quite taken up with the story. "I have never heard of him before. In our school at home I have heard of another man called Jashen. He was from the village of Gimzo in our country, a mighty warrior who fought the Philistines in the wars of our King David. In fact, he was one of the thirty bodyguards of our great king."

"I have not heard of him, Jesus, but I have heard of your King David. Strange how little we know of each other's countries and yet we are so close. David and Solomon are all that I can remember about your country. Of course," and Ari thought a moment because he did not want to offend but also wanted to be honest, "I also learned that you are a poor nation, no more than a little province in the Roman Empire. You do not have the status that Caesar and Augustus have granted the Greeks. And, I pity you, Jesus, because your people have only one God and we have many gods."

"But Ari," Jesus replied gently, "if God is God and he is Supreme, how can there be many gods?"

Ari paused a moment, gave the idea a moment's thought and quickly banished it because the idea was too new and strange for him. He felt safer on his own ground, so went on recounting what he knew about the sea.

"Whether there be a God or gods, Jesus, is too much for me."

Jesus said nothing. He knew Ari was a Thessalonian who claimed to be a Greek as most people did who wanted to get ahead in the world of learning or commerce.

"I think I know what you are thinking," Ari laughed. "Yes, I was born in Thessalonica and am proud of it. But I was educated as a Greek and am also proud of that. I guess the whole world, Jesus, is divided into two kinds of people--those who are Greek and those who want to be Greek." He laughed louder and longer.

"Ari, I like the way you laugh. They say that laughter shows we are close to God." Jesus laughed with him. "And I like your honesty."

Silently they listened to the waves lapping against the boat. Sailors were snoring, Sylvanus was muttering in his sleep.

"Good night, Jesus." Ari turned and returned to his bed roll. "I am glad you are aboard."

"Good night, Ari. I am happy we are good friends."

* * * * * *

The ship was quickly provisioned in Syracuse. There were no grain merchants on the dock. Within a few hours the *Jubilee's* sails were full blown. Captain Alexander decided the fates were with him so he charted his course through the Strait of Messina. It would save three or four days' time not going around the western coast of Sicilia. At times Alexander wondered why the trip so far had been so placid; no storms, no accidents, no lost time in port. Several times he made the remark to Ari, who said he also wondered. "The gods of Thessalonica are with us, sir," said Ari. He knew that would ruffle the captain's beard; he knew Alexander had no time for any gods.

"By Hades!" Alexander thundered, "it could not be the gods of Corinth. They bring us nothing but trouble. You should know, mate, at your age, that gods are only for children, like mermaids and monsters."

"I do not know, Captain," Ari pushed the point, "but someone or something must be responsible for our smooth sailing." He was surprised by his own remark.

Alexander dropped the subject; he did not like to think about it. He was in an expansive mood. "Get some wine, mate, and bring two mugs. Then find Jesus and tell him to come up here. I want to talk with him." Ari gladly surrendered the tiller to the captain. He found Jesus in a corner near the prow of the ship, sitting on a packing crate and a half-dozen sailors standing and sitting on the deck around him. He recalled that he often saw Jesus in recent weeks talking and laughing with the crew. He liked that.

"Young man from Nazareth," he announced with mock seriousness, "the captain wants to see you on his deck. That, I think, is a command."

Jesus excused himself as the sailors joshed him about stepping out of line and about to be flogged by the captain. Jesus laughed with them and tossed them a farewell sign.

"There you are," Alexander said as Jesus stepped up to the platform. The captain pushed aside some sailing charts and motioned Jesus to sit on the bench beside him. "I have been thinking of my son because you remind me of him. Here, take some wine Simon brought up a moment ago." He handed Jesus a mug.

"I did not know you had a son, sir."

"Indeed I do, but he disgusts me. His name is Aquila."

"You cannot really be displeased with your own son, sir. How old is he?"

"Your age. Fourteen, fifteen. He does not want to go to sea and does not want to be a sailor. How is it that you became a carpenter? With your mind I should think you would be a teacher."

"Our rabbis have a saying, sir, that says a father who does not teach his son a trade teaches him to be a thief. For that reason I think my father taught me his trade."

"Bah!" Alexander was heating up now. "That is as bad as Aquila. He wants to be a tentmaker. Imagine, a fine young man with the chance to see the world and he wants to sit in a shop and sew canvas! He is a disgrace to our family and himself. Work is for slaves—and I should know—not freedmen. I did not slave in Caesar's navy all those years to become free so that my son would be no more than a slave by his work."

"Sir, there is nothing degrading about working with your hands. Our holy books tell us that our Yahweh worked in making and adorning this beautiful world of ours. That was no mean task, sir." Jesus was trying to soothe the riled captain. "I know you do not believe in our great God, sir, but you surely must agree it is at least a point worth thinking about. Who really knows, sir, what the future holds for your son, Aquila?"

"Oh! I know what he has in mind." Alexander poured himself another mug of wine. "He has his eyes on his boss's daughter. Titus Justus, his boss, is a wealthy man. Fat chance Aquila has of ever catching her hand."

"There is a reason for everything, sir." Jesus took a swallow from his mug and continued. "Aquila might well become richer and more famous than even the great Agrippa who ruled the emperor's navy. At least, sir, why not let him chart his own course. I believe that my God governs everything and already knows what will become of Aquila."

The captain did not share the same confidence in his God but at least the words calmed him enough to enjoy the company of Jesus. "Perhaps. Perhaps. I won't live long enough to see if Aquila makes his millions. You might. But I do fear that he just might get dragged down into the sewer of Corinth."

"Captain, sir," Jesus quickly picked him up on this remark, "you surprise me when you speak that way of your city. All during your voyage you had nothing but praise for Greece and the genius of your country."

"I know, I know. But Greece is not Corinth." The captain was now in a testy mood. "But that is only because the Romans came and ruined my city. They are a voracious people, Jesus, raping their provinces of wealth and beauty and giving in return only the heavy hand of their power. Corinth now is nothing but the sewer of the world. Once it rivaled Sparta in discipline and Athens in beauty."

"Why is that, sir?" Jesus wanted to learn more.

"You have never heard of Corinth?" Alexander was surprised, then after a moment added, "How could you? Nazareth is the other side of the world! There you are safe with your parents and your one God."

"What happened to your city, Captain?" Jesus could see the sadness in his eyes and hear the homesickness in his voice.

"First, the Romans completely destroyed Corinth, about a hundred fifty years ago. They tell me there was not left a stone upon a stone."

"Someday," Jesus was thinking out loud, "I fear the Romans might do the same to Jerusalem. Go on, Captain."

"Well, even the Romans knew how strategically Corinth was located. Julius Caesar decided it should rise from its own ashes, so about fifty years ago he sent hundreds of Italic freedmen to build it up again. Just a few years ago the emperor made it the capital of Achaia and gave it a governor. But in all this process these Romans let the scum of the earth take over. Of course, you have not heard in your town about the Corinthian disease and Corinthian women. These are women of the streets, Jesus. They say there are more in Corinth than there are respectable wives. And they inflict their disease on thousands of men each year. Thieves, murderers, drunkards, addicts—all the outcasts of the world end up in Corinth. I sometimes think it would have been better if Rome had not rebuilt it and I did not go there as a freedman."

Alexander was deep in his own thoughts. The two sat in silence for several moments, the captain watching Ari at the tiller and Jesus studying Joseph and Nick as they put their heads together over several scrolls.

"Captain," Jesus said, breaking the silence, "one of our prophets, Isaiah, felt the same way about our Jerusalem about seven hundred years ago. He called its citizens 'people weighed down with guilt, a breed of wrong-doers and perverted sons.' Then one day, Captain, he had a vision and wrote it down, saying: 'Come now, let us talk this over, says Yahweh. Though your sins are like scarlet, they shall be as white as snow; though they are red as crimson, they shall be like wool.'"

"But Corinth has no such prophets, no one who can speak for its gods."

"If I were you, Captain, I would not give up on Corinth. Who knows but that someday Corinth will welcome a man even greater than our prophet, Isaiah. Who knows, but even stingy Titus Justus and your son, Aquila, might give Corinth an even greater glory than it knew in the past. Captain, our great God can do wonders even with a tentmaker."

The captain was calming down. Rudely he was brought back to his own ship. The ship's bell was clanging. Ari was calling, "All hands on deck! To the oars! The Strait's ahead!"

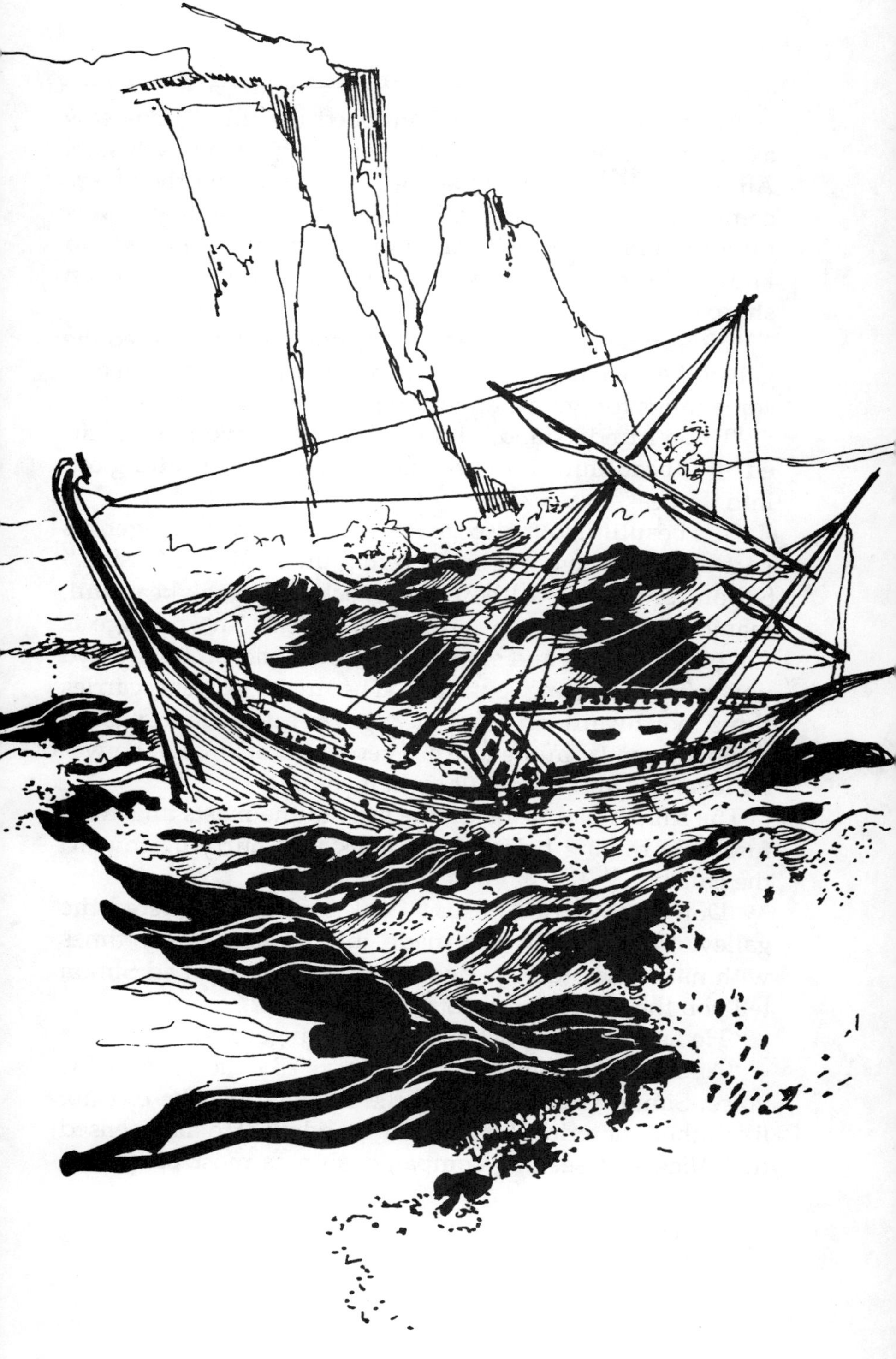

Alexander sprang up and grabbed the tiller. Jesus saw ahead a narrow passage with towering cliffs on each side. All the while they were talking neither realized they were coming so close to danger. He hurried to the galley. It was time to help Simon with the evening meal. Simon would know why the captain was so nervous and the crew on sharp alert.

"No supper tonight, son," said Simon as Jesus entered the galley. "All we'll do is set out some hardtack in a bowl and some mugs for wine if anyone has the time to catch a bite."

"I don't understand, Simon. Why is everyone so excited? It is beautiful—the cliffs, the trees, the rocks jutting out into the sea!"

"It's beautiful, but also treacherous. The most dangerous part of our voyage. We are entering the Strait of Messina." Simon continued, "Although the rocks may look beautiful, many ships have been wrecked on them. The passage is full of whirlpools and ships are pushed and pulled by two powerful, opposing currents. The main current carries ships northward and another powerful current pushes against them from the north. These currents make the water level rise and fall about eight inches."

The sailors had fastened the sails to the masts and were furiously rowing below deck. Nick was hurrying toward the galley.

"Don't be worried, Jesus," Nick said as he entered the galley. "The captain has made this passage many times with nary a scratch. He does not take chances. Did Simon tell you the history of the Strait of Messina?"

"He has told me what makes it so dangerous."

"And I am coming to the history." By the tone of his voice, Simon seemed peeved. Jesus knew that he did not like others entering his kitchen kingdom. He also sensed that Nick was seeking companionship as most people do when they are nervous about a situation. Nick sensed Simon's feelings so remained silent, but did not leave.

"The Greek poet, Homer, wrote about this strait in his poems," Simon began. "Have you heard of Homer, Jesus?"

"That rock over there," Simon was pointing to a high cliff on the starboard side of the *Jubilee*, "is the home of Scylla, a terrible monster with six heads and twelve feet that whines like a little dog. She dwells in a cave, and as ships pass by, she sticks out her head and sucks up sailors. Homer says she seized six sailors from his ship. Across from that rock," Simon pointed to a huge, flat stone, "is the home of Charybdis, another monster. She lives underneath that stone, and the legend says three times a day she sucks in all the water in the area, taking ships with it and then spouts them out like a geyser. That's why sailors say passing through the Strait of Messina between Scylla and Charybdis is like being between the devil and the deep blue sea."

"Might I suggest," Nick offered from the back of the galley, "we begin to pray to Yahweh?"

The three bowed their heads in prayer. They stood silently and solemnly as the ship was tossed to and fro, high and low, like a dead fish on the Sea of Galilee. Hours passed, then gradually the *Jubilee* settled more calmly on the waters. The sailors were slackening their pace at the oars. Jesus walked out of the galley and stood alone at the railing, gazing in admiration at the beauty all around him. He noticed seven sea gulls were trailing in the wake of the ship.

Joseph came up and stood by his side. "All the danger is passed now, Jesus. In a few days we will be in Puteoli. We must praise Yahweh for giving us safe passage. It was remarkable, Jesus. Not one accident, not one incident. Praise the Lord." Jesus looked up and smiled at Joseph.

5
The Appian Way

They had left Puteoli at sunrise and Jesus was none too sad in leaving that noisy, dirty port. To him it seemed that utter chaos was the best way to describe the malodorous city. No one seemed to talk; they all seemed to be yelling, shouting, and screaming. No one seemed to be kind to others; they were rushing and hurrying and scurrying around like a pack of rats caught in a corner of a warehouse. He thought peoople were taught to snarl there even before they cried.

It was an ugly city, with shops and offices and taverns squeezed haphazardly together along the shore like a herd of sheep at the watering hole in Nazareth. Syrians and

Greeks, Jews and Egyptians, Phoenicians and Carthagenians, sailors and merchants, thieves and cutthroats, all the dregs of humanity mingled on the wharves and streets and dark, dimly lit alleys of this sinful, shameless port. Jesus thought it must have reminded the captain many times of his own Corinth.

He noticed how the inhabitants cheered as one of Augustus' grain ships from Egypt sailed proudly with full sails into the harbor with its flags waving defiantly from its mast. It meant bread for the Romans—and money for the Puteolians. The Syrians brought with them their shameless goddess, Atargatis, who smilingly blessed every form of debauchery. The Romans and natives erected temples and shrines to their own gods of the sea, Castor and Pollux, who seemed to encourage every form of bribery, dishonesty, and corruption.

How could his people, the Jews, be faithful to Yahweh in this city of sin? Jesus put the thought aside, reassuring himself that the faithful can worship the great God and observe his Law at any time and in any place. Sadly, he thought, these poor pagan people would never be able to find God unless they had some time, some place, for silence and solitude. Then they could, if they would, discover the presence of Yahweh in their own hearts. Jesus thought of the hills surrounding Nazareth, of the pastures where he tended the sheep and goats. He knew that silence was not a luxury. He knew from his own experience as a boy that silence and solitude were necessary in order to preserve sanity and grow in sanctity.

Joseph's little band set out with a vigorous pace from the dock at Puteoli, leaving Nick in charge of the cargo. Most of the sailors were granted shore leave, with instructions to return to the ship in a fortnight. Nick kept ten sailors with him to unload the cargo at Urban's warehouse along the banks of the Tiber River in Rome. Jesus knew he would miss Nick but was happy they would meet again in Rome. He was also happy that Simon and Ari, Joseph, the Captain, and three sailors were tramping along with him in these early hours of the morning. He was happier now as the little group had left Puteoli behind them and were winding their way along the Campania road. They were gradually climbing up the hillsides that surrounded the harbor. Jesus was in good spirits as he viewed the vast orchards of orange, lemon, and apricot trees that clung to the hillsides. In some ways they reminded him of his own countryside in Galilee. From time to time he looked behind to delight his eyes with the vast expanse of azure blue water called the Tyrennean Sea.

Simon and Jesus were now bringing up the rear of the little group. For what seemed a long time to Jesus, he and Simon walked along in silence. He sensed that Simon was thinking about his family, perhaps his sons in Rome. Jesus turned his own thoughts back to Nazareth, thinking of his mother in the kitchen and Joseph in the carpenter shop. He had written them a letter while on board the *Jubilee*; Joseph told him it would be delivered in Caesarea by one of the ships returning from Puteoli in a few days. What a stir it would cause in Nazareth when his parents received it! He chuckled to himself when he thought of the curiosity it would arouse in Simon and Jude when his parents showed the letter to them!

"What are you thinking about?" Simon pierced Jesus' thoughts by his question.

"Many things, but right now about home."

"So was I," said Simon. He spoke with nostalgia in his voice.

"I was thinking of Puteoli, Simon, and how happy I am that we left it. I also wonder if people there will ever find

Yahweh when they are all so busy with making money and seeking pleasure."

"That, Jesus, is a mouthful."

By now they were far away from the port. In the distance they could see the vast fields and gardens of the wealthy Romans who chose to summer here to catch the breezes of the sea and sail their own private yachts along the coast. Jesus was happy they were now far removed from the sickly smell of sulfur that hung like a cloud over Puteoli. It was good to breathe the pure air of the Creator once again.

"Simon, how far is it to Rome?"

"About one hundred fifty miles. It should take six or seven days. We will be staying at inns along the way, but I can tell you they won't be as neat and clean as your home in Nazareth. Most probably we'll be stopping tonight at Capua."

Leading their little caravan were Joseph and Captain Alexander, setting a pace for the group that made the hare look like a tortoise. Simon explained to Jesus that Puteoli was the best and safest port that Rome had because at Ostia the Tiber constantly choked the harbor with the silt and soil it carried on its journey from the mountains to the sea. Someday he thought the Romans would develop Ostia and make it the port of Rome.

Behind Joseph, Ari followed with the three sailors. They led a mule and cart that Ari rented in Puteoli. The cart carried the special gifts Joseph had chosen for his friends and employees in Rome and the personal possessions of those in the group, including the special robe that Mary had woven for Jesus. Carefully, Simon had checked to see that the package Esther had prepared for their sons was safely tucked away in a corner of the cart.

"I am very happy," said Simon as the two kept pace behind the lead of Joeph and Alexander.

"I can see that, Simon."

"I will tell you why."

"I know, because you are going to see your sons soon."

"Yes, yes. But more than that. I have talked with Joseph many times about my boys. You know, students are always in need of money and we are not a wealthy family. Joseph said he would see what he could do and perhaps someday Urban, his agent, could find something for them. I have confidence in Joseph."

"Simon, I am happy for you and your sons. I am eager to meet them."

"If they can only get a start, Jesus, I know they will be able to make it on their own. I don't expect them ever to return to our home in Cyrene or Palestine if we retire there. But every young man needs someone to help him get a start in life. Look how your father taught you to be a carpenter."

"Why do you think they will never return home?" Jesus knew he was leading Simon on because he felt Simon wanted to talk.

"I did not tell you before that my wife is a member of your people. We have many Jews in Cyrene. They are among the finest people in our city. Esther is very devout, reading the scriptures every day and instilling the love of Yahweh in the hearts of my sons and daughters." Simon's thoughts were now far across the sea with his wife and daughters in Cyrene.

"Your wife," said Jesus, "must be as beautiful in spirit as they say our Queen Esther was in body."

"She has made me," Simon continued, "what your people call a God-fearing pagan. I, too, pray to the great Yahweh and he alone do I worship. I read the holy writings and try as best I can to follow the Law. My good wife is a

Pharisee, Jesus, and I have one problem with that."

"What is that, Simon?"

"You know I come from a people deeply influenced by Greek thought. Perhaps Ari told you, but we find it most difficult to believe that after we die we shall enter into a new life. When you're dead, Jesus, you're dead."

"Some of my people also believe that, Simon. But I do not think they read the scriptures right. These people are called Sadducees and many of them are extremely wealthy. They think Yahweh rewards people with an abundance of wealth on this earth, in this life. They do not know that Yahweh is the special friend of the poor. They really never studied the prophet Isaiah very well. You have heard the saying, 'There's no justice in this world?'"

"I've heard it and think it's true."

"But, Simon, if God is God at all he is a God of justice as well as love. We believe that all who suffer injustice will someday be vindicated. We believe that wrongs will be righted in a higher, fuller, everlasting life."

"That does make sense. Then you mean there's more to life than just this life?"

"I do, I do. Take a look around us, Simon. Day and night show us a daily resurrection; the night lies in sleep, day rises; the day departs, night takes its place. Take the harvest of these fields all around us. The farmer puts a seed into the ground. The seed dries up and seems to die. Then it pushes up a small green blade and lives again. Yahweh gives the sun and wind, the rain and the heat, and by harvest time that little seed that seemed to die gives more life than it had itself when buried in the ground."

"That's a good example, Jesus. Did I tell you that someday I hope to be a farmer?"

"A farmer?"

"Yes. I have this job with Alexander to save money, hoping someday to have enough to buy a farm, not a big one like those we see here. All I want and all Esther wants is a small piece of land, enough to live our days in peace and quiet. You know where?"

"Where?"

"In your land! Esther wants nothing more than to live near Jerusalem, to go to the Holy Temple on the great feasts, to worship Yahweh on his holy mountain. I want that too, Jesus."

"Simon, I hope you and Esther will some day have that little farm near Jerusalem. You know, God himself might have his own good reasons for having you live so close to the holy city." Jesus looked down at the huge, strong hands that Simon was swinging back and forth, back and forth.

They stopped along the road for lunch once they were in the open country. Jesus helped Simon prepare the meal. From the wagon Simon handed Jesus hard bread, cheese, and sausage which Jesus took and set on a mat he had spread out under a huge cypress tree. Ari helped Simon carry the mugs and two of the sailors brought the last goatskin of wine.

"There," said Simon with obvious relief. "This is the last good meal you'll get from my hands till we are back on the *Jubilee*." Jesus passed the bread and cheese around and Ari distributed the mugs as the two sailors poured the wine.

"With all respect for your skill, Simon, it will be good to take our meals in Urban's quarters, where his good wife and the other women add that womanly touch." Alexander stated the fact directly, without irony or humor.

Jesus handed Joseph bread and cheese and the latter smiled approvingly. "Since you have been so concerned about the emperor, Jesus, I have something here for you."

Joseph pointed to a leather folder on the ground next

to him. "You can read it now or later along the way. It is Urban's report to me about the emperor. If you have more questions, you can ask Urban when he joins us."

"Thank you, Joseph." He finished passing out the food to the others in the group but was anxious to get to the reading of the report. When he finished, he went off by himself and sat down beside a clump of wild rose bushes. He gobbled down his food, hurriedly opened the folder and within, to his surprise, was written in a fine Hebrew hand a report, not on papyrus as he expected, but on calfskin. That indicated Urban thought his report was of more than ordinary importance. He began to read the report:

> Gaius Octavius, such was the emperor's given name, was born in Velitree in the countryside of Rome seventy-two years ago. His father, a knight and later a senator, was promoted by Julius Caesar because his mother, Atia, was Caesar's niece. His father died when Octavius was still a boy. His great uncle introduced the youth to public life and later legally adopted him and made him his principal heir. Thus Octavius assumed the name of his mighty adoptive father.
>
> After the death of Julius Caesar, Octavius, a youth of eighteen, entered upon fourteen tumultuous years in his grasp for supreme power in the empire. His success can be attributed chiefly to the loyalty of Caesar's army to him and the military and naval genius of his closest friend, Marcus Agrippa.
>
> He forced Lepidius, one of the triumvirate, to retire to private life after Agrippa defeated Sextus Pompeius's naval forces. He then became sole ruler in the western part of the empire. In

the east Antony and the Egyptian queen, Cleopatra—who also dallied with Herod in Palestine—ruled supreme. Octavius knew well that only the wealth of the eastern provinces and the grain from Egypt could maintain the empire. The two lovers were a scandal even to Roman society and Octavius forced the issue of their immorality by initiating the naval battle of Actium. There Agrippa with an inferior navy defeated Antony and Cleopatra. The following year both committed suicide and Octavius became sole ruler of the empire.

Octavius was a genius at government. He was also a masterful politician, for while being a virtual dictator he maintained the appearances and trappings of a republican government.

Thirty-seven years ago the senate conferred upon him the title of Augustus, the name, as you know, which is now universally used. Although never robust in health, he suffered serious illnesses for two years, believing himself that he was at death's door. His two greatest assets, besides his native industry and ability, were his lifelong friendship with Agrippa and his faithful and devoted wife, Livia, whom he married forty-eight years ago. It is commonly reported that she is his first and most able counselor.

He has proven his genius, even though in these later years the empire seems to be at a standstill. Political observers generally point out four major achievements of his reign, namely, the establishment of a regular and constitutional government; the restoration of confidence and order throughout the Empire; the pacification of the northern frontier, even though he failed to conquer the Germanic tribes; and the beautification of Rome, even though many say this was chiefly the accomplishment of Agrippa.

No doubt, in spite of the bloody beginnings, his later years have been marked by singular progress and achievements. Thirty-nine years ago he closed the temple of Janus, the first time in two hundred years that there was no need to propitiate the Roman god of war. Twenty-three years ago, he himself built and dedicated the Altar of Peace, noting that peace reigned supreme from the rising to the setting of the sun in every part of the Empire.

The glorious triumphs of his youth have dimmed and recent events in the Empire have troubled him greatly. Last year the three-year rebellion in Illyricum was put down (although some say it is still smoldering). During the same year his valiant general, P. Quinctilius Varus, and three of the finest legions of the army were wiped out by the Germanic tribes in the Tuetoberg forest.

Adding to the disasters his armies have suffered in battle are the treasonable plots of his own family. These, they say, trouble him most because he was always conspicuous as a family man who did everything he could to strengthen the family. He had to exile his own daughter, Julia, and her daughter and son, for reasons of immorality.

Observers describe his reign—he has now ruled over fifty-three years—as cruel in its early years and mild in these latter ones. They say that today even the mighty Augustus is weary of his own cruelty.

Jesus sat for some time with the report resting in his lap. He wondered about the peace that Augustus had imposed. He would like to see that Altar of Peace and that temple of Janus. How difficult, he thought, to make a judgment of anyone and most of all about an emperor such as Augustus with the weight of the world on his shoulders. He folded the report, placed it back in the leather folder and rose to return to the group.

Jesus was more determined than ever to meet this Gaius Octavius Caesar whom people called "Divine."

* * * * * *

They arrived at the inn in Capua before nightfall. The inn was no more than a large tavern with one large room in the rear for sleeping. Jesus soon realized the establishment was not designed solely for sleeping.

The guests ranged from a frightened family with two small children from Brindisi to the rough and tumble muleteers who were raucous and rude and spent the night gambling and drinking. The food was so terrible that even the sailors said they wished Simon was back in the kitchen. The noise was incessant and Jesus longed for the peace and quiet of the Galilean hills. He stood by his mat laid out next to Joseph's and together they offered their evening prayer to Yahweh. The noise and people all around soon faded as his tired body and mind quickly surrendered to sleep.

Before the sun cast its warmth over the hills, the little band was back on the road. The Captain and Joseph were setting a faster pace today, with Ari and the sailors behind them. Jesus and Simon were bringing up the rear of the little caravan again.

"You know, Jesus," Simon was speaking hurriedly, "we left the Campania road behind us at Capua. Now we are on the Appian Road, which everybody calls 'the queen of roads.'"

Simon was in an expansive mood. Jesus could tell by the bounce in his walk and the thrust of his arms back and forth, back and forth, as they walked briskly over the huge cobblestones of the Appian Way.

"In school I heard that is what the Romans call this road, Simon, but I never really understood why." Jesus knew Simon wanted to talk and felt he wanted to talk about many things.

"The road we walk on was built over three hundred years ago by a man called Appius Claudius, so people called the road after him. He was an ancestor of the royal prince, Claudius, a cousin of Augustus."

"The Romans were great builders of roads," Jesus interrupted, recalling his days at the feet of the rabbi in Nazareth. "Our teacher taught us that the Romans came to rule the world because their soldiers marched along them. Simon, I think these same roads will someday be used to make Yahweh better known."

"Perhaps," said Simon. "Anyway, this road was built along the coast and plain to avoid the older inland road that went through the mountains. There the Roman army was once ambushed and defeated by Rome's enemy, Samnium. After this road was built, the Romans were able to conquer the Samniums. Lots of people say that because of that victory, Rome united all the tribes of Italy and went on to conquer the world. It was roads, Jesus, roads that made Rome powerful."

"These roads, then, are the cause of the peace in the world today?"

"If you want to call military might peace, Jesus, then they are. But they are also the cause of a terrible tyranny."

Simon went on to explain that the Appian road was one hundred thirty miles long between Capua and Rome. It was built mostly by the labor and death of thousands of slaves that the Roman armies captured in Dalmatia, Phrygia, and other provinces. The gray basalt paving stones were quarried out of the surrounding hillsides. In some stretches it was as straight as an arrow's flight, in other places it clung to the mountainside; in its most beautiful sections it hugged the shoreline of the Tyrennean Sea.

The life of Rome and the Empire was splashed like images on a canvas all along the road. Neighboring peasants used it as they prodded their ox-drawn carts from one settlement to another. Huge iron-wheeled wagons loaded with heavy merchandise screeched from stone to stone along the way. A traveler did not have to be on the road very long before realizing the military power of Rome. Light, skeletal iron carts carried ammunition and cannon from Rome to the ports of Puteoli or Brindisi.

Jesus met all kinds of people coming and going along the Appian Way. In many ways, it was a microcosm of the Empire. Young and exuberant students, from the noble families of Rome, accompanied by their slaves, were off to the schools of Athens, Antioch, Tarsus, and Alexandria. They appeared arrogant and supercilious. Jesus wondered if they would learn as much in these great centers as he learned in humble Nazareth. Simon told him that Cicero, the great senator, sent his son, Marcus, off to Greece to study, but the young man turned out to be more of a gambler than a student. The hard-working farmers of the countryside revealed the drudgery of their work by their silence and stoooped frames. Salesmen and businessmen whizzed by them in their horse-drawn chariots. Jesus noticed, too, the fear that fell upon all the travelers when a cohort of soldiers, under the command of their centurion, marched swiftly past them. He did not like the sound of thump-thump-thump their boots made as they struck the stones in unison. He was amazed at all the characters and animals of a circus that passed them, no doubt to put on a performance in Capua or Puteoli or some other city. Simon told him to stick close by because thieves and pickpockets made a lucrative living all along the road. From time to time he pointed out a shifty character here or a group of rowdies there who he was convinced were thieves.

As they walked along, Jesus reflected on the tyranny on which Rome built her power. All along one vast estate joined another, the domains of wealthy Romans who left their management in the hands of foremen. Some were just and honest; most were corrupt and cruel. Each estate was maintained by a thousand or more slaves; they were watched during the day by the crack of the whip and at night locked in chains. No longer was Italy the land of small farmers who helped to conquer the world. The farms were owned by absentee landowners who had become greedy capitalists. To them, money was more important than the people who earned it for them by the sweat of their brows and by the blood on their beaten backs. Jesus wondered how long slavery would continue; how long could someone keep his brother or sister in chains?

Ari dropped back from the sailors and joined them. The sky was crystal clear and the sun's rays were already beginning to bear down upon them. Ari was rejuvenated by the crisp air and was enjoying the seemingly endless miles of walking.

"Has our friend Simon been explaining the sights along the road, Jesus?" He was eager to begin a conversation.

"He has."

"And I might add, Ari, much better than you because I have made this journey more times than you." Simon was not miffed but did want Ari to know that even Cyrenians were as knowledgeable as Greeks.

"In those mountains over in the eastern sky," Ari ignored Simon's remark, "the Romans suffered one of the worst defeats in their history. About three hundred years ago they set out on conquering the world. First they had to unite Italy though, and that was no easy task. A tribe from Samnium lived in this area and was not about to surrender to the upstart Romans. At a rugged pass between those mountains, a place called the Caudine Forks, the Samniums entrapped the entire Roman army and demanded its surrender. It was a crushing, humiliating blow to Roman ambition. It took them five years to recover from that defeat."

"Jesus already knew that because I told him," Simon interjected.

Ari enjoyed talking about that Roman humiliation. He talked as if the ancient battle happened only yesterday. He relished that defeat because later the Romans conquered his beloved Thessaly.

"That was one of the reasons why Appius built this road. He also built the remarkable aqueduct we will see in a couple of days. You know the Romans have a particular love affair with water. They enjoy their baths almost every day and have fountains spouting water all over the city."

The second night they came to Formia and took lodgings at the inn there. Its guests were the same kind of people Jesus saw the night before in Capua. Poor family groups making their way to Rome; salesmen and merchants going on extended business trips from Rome; loose women, gamblers, and thieves whom Simon called the "riff-raff" of society. Jesus did not like that word, but, out of respect, he said nothing to Simon. In this inn Jesus noted the wide entrance that opened out on the street and the two wine rooms on both sides of the entrance. A lot of coarse laughter and raucous shouts came reeling out of both rooms. This night the innkeeper gave them the three bedrooms upstairs, where at least it was quieter. Perhaps Joseph bargained for these rooms. But the bedbugs, lice, and cockroaches were even more numerous than they were in Capua. Their meal in the large, common dining room made even the worst of Simon's menus look like a feast. Afterwards he went for a walk with the Captain and the three sailors.

They walked mostly in silence, enjoying the scenery all around them. Jesus smelled the orange blossoms that were in full bloom in the orchards. They walked down to the shore of the lake. Alexander explained that this was the largest lake in central Italy. The road they traveled on skirted the eastern shore of the lake to avoid the marshes between the lake and the sea.

"You will notice the sunset here, lads," Alexander spoke softly and slowly, not in his accustomed manner, "is different than any place else in the world. Its reddish glow cannot be matched any place." The sun had fallen into the water of Tyrennean Sea and the little group made its way back to the inn for the night.

The next morning Joseph again set the pace for his little band. Jesus, however, noticed that the pace had slackened; he figured that Joseph must be deep in thought about the business that awaited him in Rome.

"Where we stayed last night," Simon was speaking, "was the summer villa of Cicero. He was a staunch republican, Jesus, and vehemently opposed the imperial dictatorship of Augustus. That's why the emperor had him killed here in his villa, I suppose."

Jesus did not reply. Mile after mile he noticed the vineyards climbing up the sides of the hills. Groves of fig and olive trees stretched down to the edge of the road. Centuries ago the Romans had brought the fig trees from Syria and the olive trees from Greece. The vineyards and trees reminded him of the beauty of his Galilean countryside.

Simon told him that the builders of other Roman roads, such as the Golden Road that leads to Gaul and the Flaminia Road that winds its way to the Adriatic Sea imitated the engineering mastery of Appius. He marveled also at the graceful aqueducts along the way, marching as solid sentries in battle line across the landscape. He thought of the great works that man can accomplish when he cooperates with God in making creation more productive and useful.

The third night they stopped in Terracina. Jesus was exhausted and he knew that others in the group were also tired. They had to climb about a thousand feet up the steep incline of the hill before they came to the city. And it was a busy city! The tourist season was just beginning and Romans by the thousands were flocking to the shore of the sea stretching out below the city. Simon had told him that they were only sixty miles from Rome. Jesus noticed there were more people in the city, many of them looking like the tourists who flocked to Tiberias on the Sea of Galilee. They seemed wealthier than the people he noticed in Capua and Formia.

"Why don't we see any wealthy people in the inns?" Jesus was asking Ari as they walked toward the dining room.

"Ah! Rich people don't mingle with poor people, Jesus. They have their friends along the road and send their slaves ahead of them to alert their friends of their coming. They stay in the rich villas you noticed and they are entertained like royal princes by their hosts. Of course, when their country friends come to Rome, they have to be the hosts then."

"Another thing, Ari. I noticed many soldiers all along the road but never noticed any of them staying at the inns."

"That's because the government has a whole string of posts along the road for its military. You may have noticed the soldiers turning off the road from time to time. You don't see these military stations from the road. They're usually built a mile or two away. Old Augustus saw to it that the army is well taken care of. After all, the army supported him. But I suppose the military is always given preference by the government. At least it was that way in Sparta long ago."

Jesus retired early because he was tired. He noticed the others also retired. Simon was already asleep on his mat when Jesus entered the sleeping quarters. Tonight, however, the enemies of sleep were not so much the ribald laughter and songs of other guests, the yelling and shouting of servant boys and the screams of servant girls, as the incessant humming of mosquitoes. Their buzzing sounded angry, as if the traveler were invading their domain in the malaria-infested swamps. If angry enough, their revenge would be a sting carying the malarial germ. Other insects, like maggots and lice, allied with the mosquitoes by making the reed mats their home. They bitingly protested the invasion of their domain by intruders who were either too tired or too drunk to know enough not to use the mats. He had already found that sleeping on the ground was more comfortable than sleeping on a bed full of lice.

But Jesus did not sleep. One pesky mosquito seemed more intent on stinging him than sleeping. Jesus listened for the humming of the pest, made a futile swat with his hand and in less than a moment the buzzing started all over again. He wondered why the good Yahweh created mosquitoes. What service do they do for God or man? The mosquito bothered him even more than Simon's snoring. He heard a rap on the door.

"Yes," he whispered.

"It's Ari. I could not sleep."

"Neither can I. Wait a minute." Jesus threw his tunic over his head, picked up his sandals and went out the door as quietly as he could so he would not distrub Simon.

"I hope you don't mind me disturbing you."

"Not at all. I couldn't sleep with a mosquito as a bed

partner," Jesus was fastening his tunic about his waist.

"The mosquitoes didn't bother me so much as the foul air in our room. Let's walk."

They went out the broad entrance of the inn and walked along the cobblestone street. The moon gave them enough light to find their way. Even the noise of the city had died down by now.

"I guess I am lonesome for my family and Elaina. Do you ever get lonesome, Jesus?"

"Of course I do, Ari. I think everybody gets lonesome at times. Some of our writers say that all of us are homesick for heaven."

"I don't know about that, but tonight I feel especially lonely. All sailors get lonely, you know."

"That's why I believe King David was wise when he wrote, 'God gives the lonely a permanent home.' My people call that heaven."

They walked about the streets surrounding the inn. They did not go far away because Ari knew from experience the danger of thieves and bandits lurking in shadowy places. They did not talk much. Jesus and Ari both knew that good friends do not have to talk much. They both knew, too, that they were good friends. After an hour or so they came back to the sleeping quarters.

"Good night, Jesus, and thanks."

"Good night, Ari." Simon was still snoring as Jesus closed the door. He stretched his limbs across the blanket on the floor.

Jesus did not sleep easily, however. The temple on the cliff overlooking the city bothered him more than the mosquitoes. Captain Alexander told him at supper it was the temple of Jove, the same father-god the Greeks called Zeus. The building was massive and its architecture ponderous. Its arches looked like so many eyes spying on the little men below. These poor people, Jesus thought, know nothing about the goodness of Yahweh. You could hardly expect them, then, to know about Yahweh as our Father since even the Jews did not know that. Jesus fell asleep praying to our Father in heaven.

* * * * * *

In the morning the merchant and his followers were on the road before daybreak. Jesus sensed an air of excitement hanging over them. Simon explained that they were getting closer to Rome and that evening they would be at the inn near Three Taverns. He said Urban would be there to confer with Joseph and unfold plans he had made for their stay in Rome. Simon was excited because he knew the next day he would see his sons.

"You are very happy, Simon."

"Right you are, my son. I shall soon see Rufus and Alexander. I am sure Urban will inform them of our coming."

"But Urban is not a Jew, is he?"

"No, but he is God-fearing like myself. It is difficult for a Jew to conduct business with the Gentiles in Rome, Jesus. That is why Joseph has employed him as his agent. He is a good man, an honest man, and in Joseph's business honest men are few."

Jesus was beginning to catch the fever of excitement. He knew he must talk to Joseph before the merchant became too involved with his business affairs. He excused himself and told Simon he was going ahead to visit with Joseph. He paused on his way to greet Ari and joke with the sailors. He noticed how their gait had quickened and their talk and laughter were louder.

"Joseph, if you are not too busy I have some things to ask you about." Jesus fell into step with Joseph and Alexander.

"Good morning, my young friend. I see that you are becoming just as eager as the rest of us."

"I am."

"You would be a dull lad indeed if you did not." This from Alexander. "I know your eyes will be bulging tomorrow, Jesus. Nothing you have ever seen in your little country can compare with what you will see in Rome."

"Tell me, Jesus, why are you so anxious? What do you want to know?" Joseph noticed that the young man seemed more serious and grave than usual.

"I am wondering, Joseph," Jesus spoke slowly and surely, "if we will see the emperor."

"Oh! My young friend! Is that what wrinkles your brow? Are you afraid of him?" Joseph seemed troubled because Jesus looked so serious.

"Not at all, Joseph. I do not fear him but want very much to meet him."

"Then I know you will be disappointed. I told you, Jesus, very few people ever see Augustus and even fewer ever talk to him. He is a solemn, silent man and seldom appears in public. Urban once told me that in all his life he had only seen the emperor once."

The threesome fell into silence. The road skirted the ocean and Jesus could hear and see the waves lapping against the shore. He smelled the salt in the air and knew that would enliven the spirit of Alexander. He noticed the canal the emperor had recently constructed. Little donkeys were drawing barges and pleasure crafts over its waters. He knew, though, they would not use the canal because Joseph's thriftiness prevented him from indulging in what he considered a luxury.

The Pontine marshes were far behind them. They were approaching the Alban hills. Jesus marveled at the beauty of the countryside, the greenery that decorated the sides of the hills and the tiny villages clinging to them or perched like some golden bird on their summits. They were making a steeper ascent now and Jesus could hear the squeaking of the wheels on the cart. He was not in the least tired and did not feel any exertion.

He knew that Joseph was deep in thought. He recalled all the events, all the experiences, all the wonders and strange new people and places he had seen along the journey during the past month. What stories he would have to tell his parents, his cousins and friends in Nazareth! Marvelous as everything had been, he still had only one goal in mind: He must see Caesar Augustus!

They walked on in silence and he heard the heavy breathing of the captain. He knew that even though his people were God's chosen people, God's mercy was boundless and God desired that all people would come to see him face to face. Surely, Yahweh, with whom all things were possible, would bring to new life a noble pagan such as Alexander. The words of the psalmist came to mind and he prayed as he walked along:

> For Yahweh is a great God,
> a greater King than all other gods;
> from depths of earth to mountain top
> everything comes under his rule;
> the sea belongs to him, he made it,
> so does the land, he shaped this too.

6

The Inn of the Three Taverns

The commotion was so great it bordered on chaos, but there was a happy, holiday mood. Silvanus, the innkeeper, stood grinning from cheek to fat cheek when he was not bawling out an order now to one servant and next to another. Urban was walking back and forth, trying to look busy, but his joy in seeing Joseph and the little caravan got in the way of his ploy. Servants scurried in one door and out the other. If one did not know better, he would conclude, as Jesus was thinking right now, that Silvanus's establishment was poorly managed. Jesus did not know better as he stood in amazement inside the entrance of the courtyard.

Simon touched his arm. "Don't be afraid. It is always like this. Silvanus and Urban are brothers and Joseph is one of their closest friends. Urban came out from the city yesterday to make sure that everything would be ready for Joseph's arrival."

Ari and the sailors were being led away by a handful of stable boys who were leading the donkey and the cart through an arch on the north side of the courtyard. They knew what they were doing.

"I am not afraid, Simon," Jesus replied. "I am just surprised. This is not like the other inns where we stayed. When you mentioned Three Taverns I thought that was the name of the inn and it would be rowdier than any of the others."

"Thought so. Thought so. Three Taverns, Jesus, is the name of the village which took its name many years ago from the three different taverns in this area. This inn is called the King's Way in honor of Yahweh, for Silvanus is a God-fearing Gentile like Urban. Silvanus operates the best inn along the Appian Way. His servants know exactly what they are doing. You will see how well they will provide for all of us."

"Jesus, over here!" Joseph was calling. "Come meet our friends." Jesus strode across the courtyard, Simon walking beside him. He could not believe the two strangers he saw standing next to Joseph were brothers. The one, who he soon learned was Silvanus, was short and round and looked as if you gave him a push he would roll rather than stumble. The other was tall, thin, strikingly handsome, with two shining eyes piercing through dark, bushy eyebrows and velvet black hair descending into a black, bushy beard. Jesus judged both of them to be in their mid-twenties.

"Silvanus," Joseph said, "this is my young friend, Jesus of Nazareth in Galilee. For his age he is learned in the Law and the history of our people."

"I am pleased to meet you," said Jesus.

"And I, you. This is my brother, Urban. If you need anything, Jesus, you can blame Urban. He has made the arrangements."

"A friend of Joseph is a friend of mine," said Urban, and he embraced Jesus. He turned and embraced Simon as his brother had already done.

"Urban, I must tell you that our young friend should see as much of Rome as he can while we are attending to business. I hope you have found some worthy companions for him." Joseph had already made arrangements for what would happen next. He said this with a glint of joy in his eyes.

"By all means, Joseph," said Urban. "I have found two of the finest young men to act as his guides." He turned to the central part of the inn and called, "Rufus! Alexander! Come quickly."

Two youths bounded out of the building, running hurriedly toward Simon. Jesus turned toward Simon, standing frozen like a cold marble statue. He mumbled in disbelief, "Rufus! Alexander!" The youths fell upon their father with hugs and embraces and kisses. Questions tumbled out about mother and home and sisters and friends and...

"Now, now, now, not so fast," Simon regained his composure. "First, we must thank Joseph, and you, Urban, for this great surprise. How did you?...How could you?..."

"Simon, it was not in the least bit difficult," Joseph began the explanation.

"My apologies, Joseph, for myself and my sons. This is my younger son, Rufus, and this is Alexander. This man, Joseph, is our great benefactor. Go and greet him." The boys approached Joseph and he warmly embraced both of them.

"I knew that Urban needed some help in the warehouse, Simon," Joseph was now able to continue his explanation, "so I wrote and asked him to locate your sons and make them apprentices in our firm. I also knew that if they were as good as their father—and I will see that in the next few days, boys—they would serve as good guides for Jesus."

The two approached Jesus, who said to each, "Shalom!" and they, to his surprise, replied, "Shalom!"

"And it was not difficult for me in locating you two." Urban picked up the conversation. "In the Roman Academy of Rhetoric there are not many students from Cyrene.

So, Joseph, I have already employed them. They are starting from the ground up."

"And that means sweeping the floors, father," said Alexander. He laughed and everyone chuckled.

"Come, come now," Silvanus interrupted. His voice always seemed to have a booming ring while his brother, Urban, spoke softly and slowly. "Let us get you settled into your rooms and then we can all gather for the dinner the cooks have prepared." He clapped his hands and, as if out of nowhere, a half-dozen servants appeared. They stood on the perimeter of the small circle, awaiting their orders.

The servants had been well instructed beforehand. Silvanus read from a list he held in his hand and assigned the rooms. "Joseph and Alexander will use the room named 'Iris'; Aristarchus and Simon, in the room called 'Lily'; the sailors, Ignatius, Barbus, and Archimedes, in the 'Poppy' room; Rufus, Alexander, and Jesus in the room of the 'Rose.'"

"Now, now," Silvanus continued, sounding like a drill sergeant in the emperor's army, "off with you. Wash up, rest a bit, and be in the dining room in an hour."

The servants headed for the cart, waiting to be instructed to take the baggage for each guest. They had already been assigned to serve the various guests.

One of the servants approached Jesus. "May I be of assistance, sir?" Jesus was taken aback. The man did not seem to be much older than himself. He spoke with a crude accent and his features were definitely not like the Romans Jesus had seen.

"Pardon me," the youth repeated; "may I help you, sir?"

"I am sorry," Jesus replied quickly. "I do not think I need any help. I have only a handful of possessions and can get them from the wagon myself."

"Begging your pardon, sir," the youth was well trained in his duties, "you would do me a disservice if I could not get them for you."

"Very well, by all means," Jesus replied. "Let us get them together." They walked toward the cart, which was now in a little corral next to the barn beyond the gate on the northern side of the courtyard. As they walked together, the servant walking one step behind Jesus, they became acquainted.

"What is your name, my friend?"

"I am Argentius," he replied, adding politely, "sir."

"You are not a Roman, are you?"

"No, sir."

"Neither am I, for my home is in Nazareth in Galilee."

"I am from Gaul," said Argentius, "and I lived near Treves before I was captured by the Roman army and sold as a slave to Silvanus. I am fortunate to have so kind a master."

"My name is Jesus; please call me that, Argentius." Jesus was perplexed. He had never before met a slave and the whole idea of slavery he detested. He recalled the many passages in the sacred books that told of the slavery of his own people. In his very blood he still felt the affliction his ancestors suffered in Egypt. The words from the Law flashed through his mind: "The sons of Israel, groaning in their slavery, cried out for help and from the depth of their slavery their cry came up to God. God heard their groaning and he called to mind his covenant with Abraham, Isaac, and Jacob."

"I detest slavery, Argentius. I am sorry for you"

"No need, Jesus, to feel sorry for me. I consider myself fortunate, fortunate indeed. I have a good master. If I am faithful to him, one of these years he will give me my freedom. He has already freed dozens of his slaves."

Jesus scratched his head in puzzlement. He believed firmly that only Yahweh gives freedom and no man should bow his neck to a brother man. "I do not understand, Argentius, but I am happy if you are happy. There," he pointed to a small goatskin bag that his mother had carefully packed, "there is my bag."

"Come, now, let's get settled for the night." Alexander was speaking to Jesus as he and Rufus joined the young man from Galilee and the young man from Gaul. The foursome walked toward the room of the Rose with Argentius leading the way. Alexander was studying Jesus, noting that he was several inches taller and darker in complexion.

He had never seen such composure in any of his friends at the academy.

"I am amazed at you, Jesus," Rufus now spoke.

"Why is that, Rufus?"

"Why don't you call me Ruf and Alexander, Alex. All our friends do. My father wrote and told us that you were his assistant aboard the *Jubilee*. He told us, too, that you are a friend of Joseph of Arimathea and yet no more than the son of a carpenter as we are no more than the sons of a ship's cook. He told us you helped him a great deal. I agree with my father that it is a very, very strange world."

"Your father, Ruf, is a very kind man who has been very good to me." Jesus was picking his words, for he knew Ruf wanted more of a reply and he was not quite sure of what more he could say. "Your father someday may help me more than I ever helped him."

Ruf did not understand these strange words. He stood speechless for a moment.

"Hurry up," said Alex as he gave Ruf a gentle push. The threesome followed Argentius as he led them through the great dining hall, down a narrow portico until they came to a door that faced the western expanse that gradually faded into the distance.

"Here we are," said Argentius. He opened the door and added, "I trust that you will find the accomodations satisfactory."

"They are," said Ruf.

"Thank you very much, gentlemen."

Jesus surveyed the room at a glance. Four pallets of fresh, clean straw were laid out in each corner of the room. Against the far wall stood a writing desk and chair. Between the two pallets on the eastern wall a pitcher and wash basin rested on a small table, and next to them a stack of clean, white, linen towels. He had not seen such cleanliness since he left the *Jubilee*.

"I will call you ten minutes before supper," said Argentius. He closed the door and left. The three stood awkwardly in the middle of the room.

"Since I am the oldest," said Alex, "I will wash first."

"That's because you need it the most," Ruf said jokingly. He walked toward one pallet on which a newly woven toga trimmed with golden thread was neatly folded. "This is for you, Jesus." He pointed at the toga.

"But I already have a tunic in my bag that was woven by my mother for this journey."

"When in Rome you may someday have to dress as a gentleman." Ruf walked toward him as Alex was splashing water over his face and on the floor. "Everyone wears a tunic," Ruf continued, "even slaves. Julia, a close friend of Urban, heard of your coming and wove this toga for you. She kept saying the past weeks that she felt someday in Rome you will have need for it."

"When I meet Julia, I must thank her," Jesus replied. He lifted the toga, unfolded it, and measured it beside his own stature. "Ruf, I don't even know how to wear this garment. I have never seen anything like it in Galilee."

Ruf took the toga from Jesus' hands. It was a circular garment about six feet in diameter with a hole in the middle and a golden band around the entire piece of cloth.

"Let's try it on for size," said Ruf. He placed the garment over Jesus' head and it fell like a tent around him. "You must gather up all these folds," Ruf laughed and Alex joined in the laughter from the wash stand. "Hold them in your elbows. There, that's the way. Strange that Julia should trim the toga with that golden band."

"Why is that?" Jesus asked.

"Because, as far as I know, most Roman citizens wear plain white togas with no embroidery or color. They really do not like to wear them. But the emperor had decreed at all important functions gentlemen must wear togas. Only members of the Senate wear togas with bands of purple around their edges to distinguish themselves from the others."

"It was thoughtful of Julia to add the golden bands. Perhaps she wanted to show that a Jew comes from the land of a golden, rising sun."

"Perhaps," said Ruf.

"Next," said Alex. He stretched out on his pallet as the other two washed themselves.

After a short rest, Argentius knocked on the door and led them into the large, spacious dining hall with the windows on the other side catching a last glimpse of the setting sun. Tables were set for two, four, eight, twelve, and twenty, covered with linen cloths and placed in various areas of the room. There was still enough sunlight to embrace the room in a warm amber glow. Later the candles on the walls and tables would be lighted.

"Here, here!" cried Silvanus. He motioned the young men to a table set for twelve in a far corner of the room. Jesus and the brothers walked across the dining room and stood beside their host. "There," motioned Silvanus, "you, Alex, and you, Ruf, take your places beside your father. There, Jesus, take your place beside Ari." Argentius took his place, standing behind Jesus' chair. Joseph, Alexander, Urban, and the three sailors were already in their places. Urban was sitting next to Joseph. "Now," said Silvanus, obviously enjoying playing host and very much aware of who his chief client was, "we invite you, Joseph, to call down the blessing of Yahweh upon this company and this food."

Without the slightest embarrassment, and with the least ostentation, Joseph rose and all around the table also rose.

Joseph bowed his head, as did most of the guests, and after a moment's silence, prayed:

> Give thanks to the Lord because he is good;
> his love is eternal.
> Give thanks to the greatest of all gods;
> his love is eternal.
> Give thanks to the mightiest of all lords;
> his love eternal.
> He alone performs great miracles;
> his love is eternal.
> By his wisdom he made the heavens;
> his love is eternal.
> He built the earth on the deep waters;
> his love is eternal.
> He made the sun and the moon;
> his love is eternal.
> The sun to rule over the day;
> his love is eternal.
> The moon and the stars to rule over the night;
> his love is eternal.

Joseph paused. Those around the table answered, "Amen." Argentius stood silently, amazed at this public prayer to a God who was no stranger to him even though he was a stranger to this God.

Silvanus turned to the servants, "Bring on the food. Our guests are hungry." The food came forth, brought by six servants in amounts and varieties that Jesus had never seen before. They carried in fresh fruits, pears, figs, and oranges; a tray of seafood, pasta cooked in tomatoes and mushroom sauce; a roasted mutton just taken from the spit; fresh salad of lettuce, chives, spinach, and beet leaves with oil and vinegar; last of all, a table of cakes and cookies and undreamed of creations with whipped cream, cherries, nuts, and candies. There were red wines and white wines, wines from the nearby hills and wines from Syria. Jesus did not know before this night that such foods and sweets even existed.

"Simon," Ari exclaimed at one point, "this makes up for all the hardtack and smoked fish we ate on the *Jubilee!*"

"But we were on ship," Simon hastily replied. "I never had the whole countryside as my pantry."

So the banter went on. Merriment marked the entire evening. At one point Jesus overheard Urban say to Joseph, "Sir, I already have a consignment that will more than fill the *Jubilee* on its return to Caesarea. Business has been very active this spring."

"Not now, Urban, not now." Joseph brushed the remark aside. "Tomorrow and the next days we can talk business. Nick will be with us then. Tonight, we relax and thank God for the approaching end of our journey."

"My young friend from Nazareth," Urban turned toward Jesus, "did you find in your room the gift I brought for you?"

"I did, Urban, and I am most grateful. I think your friend, Julia, is trying to make a Roman out of me!"

"They say, Jesus, when in Rome do as the Romans. I hope you will find some use for the toga in the coming days."

"Well, well," Silvanus boomed, "more *dulci*. Help yourselves. There is much more where it comes from." But the guests had their fill and expressed thanks to Silvanus and Joseph. Joseph gave the signal that dinner was over. The servants began clearing off the table. Argentius knew his place; he helped the servants and retired with them to the kitchen.

After dinner the little group began to split into smaller

bands. Silvanus led Joseph and Urban to a small parlor adjacent to the dining hall. Simon invited Jesus to join him and his sons on a walk around the town, but Jesus declined. They would have much to talk about their family and friends in Cyrene. The sailors had already disappeared, no doubt in search of an inn where they might find more pleasures to their liking.

Ari approached Jesus. "How do you like your room with Alex and Ruf?"

"It is the finest I have ever seen," said Jesus, "and I like both of them very much."

"I think you like everyone, Jesus, and I know everyone likes you."

"Yahweh tells us, Ari, that we should love others as we love ourselves."

"Then you must have pity on me, for I share my room with Simon and he snores louder than Zeus roars on Olympus!"

"I did not know that Zeus roared," Jesus laughed. So did Ari.

"It's only a figure of speech. You know very well that I do not really believe in Zeus or any of the other gods."

"For that, not Simon's snoring, I pity you. It must be a terrible life to live without knowing the one true God."

"Oh, sometimes I think there is some sort of god out there; most Greeks do, you know. Even our old philosophers like Plato and Aristotle realized there had to be some cause of everything, someone or something that set this weary old world in motion. What is your God like, Jesus?"

"That is a difficult question to ask standing here in this hall. Let's go out in the garden. At home my mother and father and I often sat at night watching the setting sun playing shadow games against our Galilean hills."

They walked through the huge archway they had entered when first coming to the inn. They entered a garden which was filled with the scent of flowers in bloom. They sat on a bench next to a marble fountain whose waters splashed from the top to the lower of its three tiers before falling into the small pond on the ground.

"You love your mother and father very much, don't you?"

"I do. Not a day goes by that I do not think of them. You love your parents, too?"

"I am sure I do," he replied. He stooped over and plucked a deep yellow rose from its prickly branch. "But I do not think Greeks have as much devotion to their parents and family as you Jewish people do. We are taught very young to stand on our own two feet and look after ourselves. I suppose it is the influence of the militaristic spirit of the Spartans."

"For my people love of family is close to love of God," said Jesus. "One of the ancient writers wrote,'Long life comes to him who honors his father, he who sets his mother at ease is showing obedience to the Lord. He serves his parents as he does his Lord. Respect your father in deed as well as word, so that blessing may come on you from him; since a father's blessing makes the house of his children firm.'"

"Who is your God, Jesus?" Ari was moved by the words of Jesus.

"First, I must tell you, Ari, the Jewish people attach a great deal of importance to a name. For them a name signifies much more than just a random grouping of letters."

"Then, what is the name of your God?"

"Sometimes we call him 'Elohim,' which means 'the true God above all other gods.' In prayer we address him as 'Elohim' or 'Eloi,' as in a prayer, 'Eloi, Eloi, lama sabachthani.'"

"And what does that mean?"

"It expresses a cry for help when all help seems impossible. We believe that help will come from 'Eloi,' the true God above all other gods."

"That is not a prayer, then, but a cry of desperation."

"Not in the way we use it, though. David our king used it in one of his songs. It is really the cry of a good and holy man who finds his consolation and victory over all troubles in the certain knowledge of our God's approval."

"I see. And what other words do you use to talk to your God?"

"Sometimes we address him as 'Shaddai,' which means he is 'the Highest and Most Exalted.' Then we also call him 'Adonai' because he is our Lord and we depend on him for everything."

"What you have, then, is many names for your God, instead of many gods."

"That is true, Ari. But the most solemn, the most holy, and the name our God used is 'Yahweh.'"

"And what does that name mean, Jesus?" Ari was intrigued by the conversation. Jesus noted the wonderment in his eyes and went on.

"Our God has this great and holy name because he called himself Yahweh when he revealed himself to our great law-giver, Moses. It means our God is absolute and unchangeable, infinite in perfection and power. I believe that is how your Greek philosophers would say it."

"When did he tell this name to Moses?" Ari spoke in a hush.

Jesus told Ari how God appeared long ago on Mount Horeb. He spoke from a burning bush that was not consumed by fire. He commanded Moses to deliver his people from the slavery they suffered under the Egyptians. Moses asked this voice from the bush who he was, and the voice replied he was the God of Abraham, Isaac, and Jacob. Moses asked the voice if the people asked him who sent him what name should he give them. Then our God revealed his name: I am who I am. Yahweh.

They sat in silence for what seemed a long time. Ari was moved; never had he heard how close a god had come to man. Jesus knew his friend was thinking deeply. The noise of the village could be heard in the background. The servants of Silvanus were lighting the torches in the courtyard. The stars were lighting up the deep blue blanket of the sky.

Ari cleared his throat. "How I wish, Jesus, that I could believe in 'I am who I am.' He must be the greatest God that ever could be when he could come so close to a man like Moses."

"Someday I am sure you will." Jesus placed his hand on his friend's arm. "You will come to believe also a greater prophet and teacher than Moses. Then, Ari, your life will be changed."

"If you do not mind, Jesus, I will begin tonight to pray to your God for that gift."

"And he will hear you. Have no doubt about that."

Urban came strolling into the garden. He had left Joseph and Silvanus talking and saw the two sitting on the bench. He walked toward them with long strides and a firm step. He was a man sure of himself and firmly in control. Joseph had chosen his agent wisely.

"There you are, Jesus. We have hardly had a moment to talk. Joseph has been telling me many good things about you."

"Joseph is a very kind man," Jesus said as he rose to greet Urban.

"He told me that he gave you the report about the emperor that I had drawn up for him. Did you find it of some interest?"

"Very much, and I have some questions I hope to ask you in the next few days."

"No time like the present, they say."

"And I beg to be excused." Ari rose from the bench and added, "I fear I am not much interested in the emperor of the Romans. I have much to think about now." He walked toward the archway, walking slowly like an old man carrying a heavy burden on his back.

"I did not mean to interrupt you," Urban said.

"Not at all. We were just talking."

"Shall we talk, then? There is a little stream over there. It meanders through a wooded area and it is very peaceful and quiet. We will not be disturbed by lovers, or rather, we will not disturb them because it is still quite early."

"I like that very much." Jesus followed behind Urban. The moon was slowly rising over the Alban hills, appearing as if the large yellow disk were coming out of the very center of the highest hill.

"This is the time of the spring equinox, Jesus. For the Romans it is a time of games and feasting, and I must also admit, much debauchery and crime." Urban pointed in the direction of a path that began under a deep green magnolia tree.

"Simon told me of these revelries," Jesus replied. "At home we have a saying about them."

"And what is that?"

"For festivals the Jews go to the temple and the Romans go to the games."

"That, I believe, is true. Now, what was it you wanted to know about Augustus?" They were strolling leisurely side by side. The silence of the evening was interrupted only by the muffled sounds of little creatures of the forest scurrying here and there.

"In your report, Urban, you did not mention what the

emperor looked like."

"Well, I did not think that was too important." Urban picked up a small stone and began gently tossing it from one hand to the other. "Yours, my friend, is really two questions."

"How is that?"

"If you mean how he looks today, I can answer that, for I did get a good look at him several years ago when he officiated at the Altar of Peace. But I did not put that in my report. If you mean how he looked as a younger man, I can only tell you what others have told me."

"How does he look today, Urban? I am more interested in that."

"You must remember, he is an old man, seventy-three I believe. His hair, which was once light brown, has turned a pale yellow color, although it is still curly. His teeth are decayed, widely separated, and almost brown. His ears are rather small and his long aquiline nose bends inward at the bottom. He stands only five and a half feet tall, and they say he walks with a limp. In his youth he was an exceptionally handsome young man by Roman standards and his good looks have not completely disappeared. Now, does that answer your question?"

"Very much so. He is, then, not like my people who are more dark and swarthy. You also have a light complexion, Urban, and light brown hair and blue eyes. Are you a Roman?"

"All my life, and proud of it, Jesus. My father's house is only five blocks from mine and there I was born. I have spent all my life in the same neighborhood near the Tiber River. Did I tell you, though, than many of my friends are Jewish?"

"I guessed that, Urban."

"Many Jewish people—they say about five thousand—

live in my neighborhood. Most of them are shopkeepers, some merchants with fine, elegant stores who cater to the extremely wealthy people."

"Has Augustus been good to the Jews in Rome?"

"Indeed he has. He was a friend of your King Herod and no doubt that friendship influenced his policy. He has exempted them from the obligation of all Roman citizens to worship the gods. He allows them to send their temple tax to Jerusalem each year. I really believe that he secretly admires them."

"Why do you say that, Urban?"

"There are many people in Rome, Jesus, especially among the learned and wealthy, who admire the Jews for their worship of only one God. And even if they do not observe them, they admire the ten commandments your great Moses gave your people. I am sure that Augustus shares that admiration."

"You would say, then, that Augustus is a religious man?"

They had come to a little stream and its fresh, clear water was bouncing against the pebbles in its shallow bed. Urban took his stone and made it hop and skip over the water. A young couple locked arm in arm was approaching them.

"This stream, Jesus, is fed by the snows that fall on the Alban hills there in the east. By July it will be dry, thirstily waiting for nature to give it new life next spring."

"I have been watching those hills all day, Urban. They remind me of the mountains that surround my own village."

"Joseph told me that's a little town called Nazareth. You are a Galilean, then?"

"Yes. But I was not born in Nazareth. Bethlehem in Judea is my birthplace, and I am a member of the house of David."

"Joseph did not tell me that."

"I do not think he knows. At least he never asked."

"How was it that you were born in Bethlehem?"

"Your emperor, Urban." Jesus laughed and Urban looked puzzled.

"And what would the mighty Augustus have to do with the birth of a little Jewish baby in Bethlehem?"

"Your Augustus ordered a census of the empire, and my father, whose name is also Joseph, and my mother had to take the road to Bethlehem to be enrolled. There I was born fourteen years ago."

"Augustus was a fanatic on taking census. We have already had three of them during his reign. He and his governors are always counting heads. Tax purposes, you know."

"I have come to Rome to see him."

"Now wait a minute, Jesus. It is perfectly all right to be interested in Augustus. Most people are. But you will never see him. He is a shy man. He seldom appears in public."

"How is the emperor a religious man, Urban?" Jesus ignored the last remark.

"I told you that like many others he admires the ten commandments. Much of this morality he has tried to put into the laws of the Empire. Of course, he has not succeeded, but at least on the books he tries to maintain the sacredness of the family."

"For that he deserves to be admired and praised."

"And he does not believe in the Roman gods any more than any other intelligent person. And he knows better than anyone that he is not divine."

"Why, then, does he officiate at ceremonies as the Chief High Priest of the Empire and even allow people to call him 'Augustus'?"

"It is simple, Jesus. His god is the state and in his person he believes he embodies the whole empire."

"In other words," Jesus said slowly, almost as if speaking to himself, "he has made a god out of the state. I feel sorry for him and everyone who thinks like him."

They had left the little creek behind them and were coming out of the woods. The lights of the inn could be seen in the distance and the sound of voices was becoming louder. "What do you think of this mighty Augustus, Urban?"

"I think he will go down in history as one of the world's greatest men, Jesus." Urban paused a moment and continued. "He has brought some kind of peace to the world and that is one of man's greatest gifts."

"I must see him, Urban, and thank him, for I was born under his rule, when, as you said, the whole world was at peace."

Urban was moved by the seriousness of his new friend. He shrugged it off. "Come, let us join our friends."

He patted Jesus on the back and they walked into the inn for the night.

7

The Center of the World

Jesus bade farewell to Argentius and thanked him for his help. Silvanus was no more than a shadow standing in the entrance of the inn as Joseph and the little band started before sunrise.

"It is thirty-three miles to Rome," Joseph explained, "and we want to reach Urban's quarters tonight. It will be a long, hard day, Jesus, because we will be winding our way around the Alban hills."

The group trudged along in silence during these early hours of the day. Ari was mulling over in his mind all that he and Jesus had talked about last night. Even Alex and Ruf were subdued as they walked along beside Jesus and their father. Jesus noticed that Joseph had set a fast pace. From time to time one of the sailors rapped a willow stick over the buttocks of the mules to hurry them along.

A soothing breeze made the walking easier as they followed the road up one side and down the other side of the hills. The sun had risen and warmed the bodies of the travelers. The road was filling up with more and more people, going to and coming from Rome. Many wealthy men whizzed past them in their flashy, horse-drawn chariots.

As they walked along, Simon began the conversation, explaining to Jesus what he would see along the road in the coming hours. He explained that they would most probably stop for lunch along the road overlooking Lake Albano, which was all that remained of a volcano many centuries old. He pointed out the aqueduct that Appius built, which was a major source of water for the thirsty Romans. He said they would pass by many ornate tombs along the road as they drew closer to the city. Romans built these mounuments to honor the deceased members of their families. Simon said he thought they really built them to show off their own wealth and power. One of the most elaborate of all the tombs was that of Cecilia Metella, about two miles outside the walls of the city. She was a "mystery woman," Simon said. All that people said about her was she was a close associate of a wealthy friend of Julius Caesar.

So the time passed. The group did stop, as Simon said, in a grove of cypress trees overlooking Lake Albano. Jesus noted that it was not at all like the Sea of Galilee; it was very beautiful with its deep blue water and surrounded by the hills covered with many shades of green of the trees and shrubs. The rest break was brief and the group was on its way.

Jesus stood on the summit of the hill, his eyes filled with wonderment. Never, not even in holy Jerusalem, nothing, not even the beauty of his beloved Galilean hills, filled him with such awe.

Alex was standing by his side but did not speak for some time. He wanted Jesus to be able to drink in the panorama just as he had done the first time he came to Rome. "This is Rome, eternal Rome!"

"Never did I dream a city could be so beautiful. I always thought Jerusalem was the most beautiful city in the world."

"I don't know about that," Alex replied, "because I have never seen Jerusalem. My mother often talked about it, though, because she had been there once. From what she said, I think Jerusalem is beautiful because of its holiness. Rome's beauty is more external because it is based on power and wealth."

Joseph, Urban, Simon, and Ari had joined the three young men on the hilltop. On every journey over the immense stones of the Appian Way, this little group of Joseph's stopped here to view Rome. It was always a thrilling and breathtaking sight. The road lay beneath them, winding its way in what seemed a helter-skelter manner, twisting and turning down the side of the hill until it appeared again as a deep purple band of ribbon rolled across the plain.

"How many people live in this metropolis?" Ari addressed the question to Urban.

"No one really knows for certain. They say about a million people."

"A million people!" Ari blew a loud, shrill whistle. "It doesn't look that big."

"I know, it surprises everyone. But you see, Ari, the city goes up rather than out. When we come closer, you will see that many of the buildings almost scrape the sky."

CENTRAL ROME

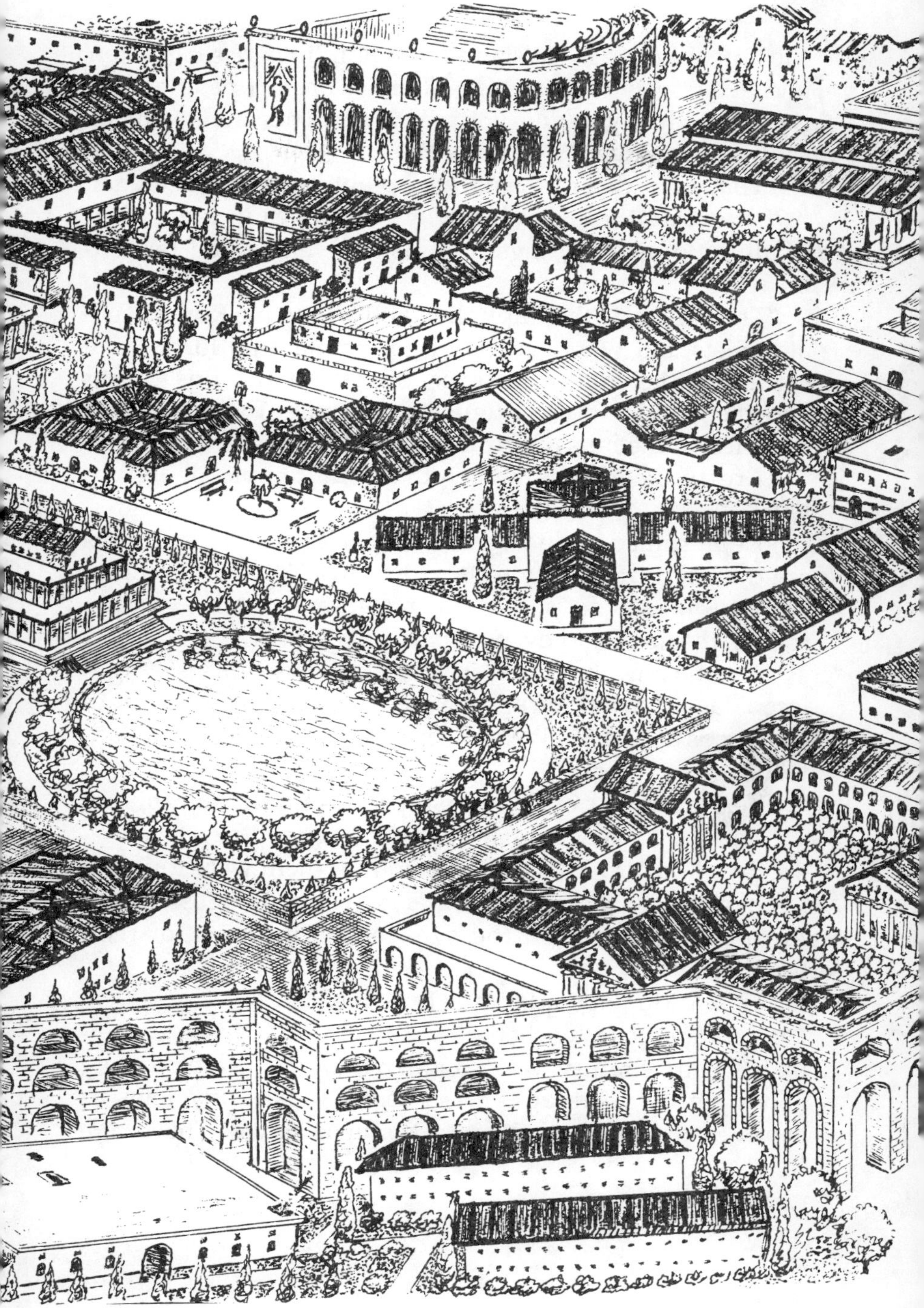

Most people live in flats and these buildings rise eight, ten, and even twelve stories high. Romans are not people in little houses like you and your family in Thessalonica or Joseph in Arimathea."

"That area there," Jesus was pointing with his finger, "what are all those shining white buildings in the middle of all the other buildings that look so yellow and tan and brown?"

"That, Jesus, is the Capitoline Hill where the Roman senate meets and where edicts of government go forth to all corners of the empire. You see, the forum of Julius Caesar and the new forum of Augustus are built of white marble quarried in the hills of Carrara north of Rome."

"Are those forums bigger than our temple in Jerusalem?"

Joseph smiled. "Much, much bigger, Jesus. These forums are the heart of the city for the Romans. There are temples there to false gods, shops and restaurants, baths, reading rooms, theaters, and even a library."

"Is not Yahweh adored in Rome and his praises sung?" Jesus' face showed his perplexity. No youth from Nazareth could possibly conceive a place where the praises of Yahweh were not sung.

"Yes, Jesus, our God is worshiped here," Urban replied.

"There is a synagogue in Rome?"

"By all means. Two of them. Both of them were founded by freedmen who were former slaves of Augustus and Agrippa. They named the synagogues in honor of their two patrons."

"How did my people come to Rome?"

"Perhaps your teachers never told you," Urban continued. "Your country was conquered by the Roman army about eighty years ago. The general took many Jews as captives and shipped them to Rome as slaves. They were peaceful slaves, causing no trouble, and thus many of them were freed by their masters. That was the beginning of the Jewish community in Rome."

"And the Gentiles do not persecute them?"

"So far, no. The Jews are respected for their peaceful way of living, their industry, and their talents."

Jesus was pleased that there were two synagogues in Rome. "How many Jews live in Rome, Urban?"

"About five thousand."

The group began the descent of the hill and continued its march across the plain. By the time the sun was stretching its long shadows against the walls of the city, the travelers passed through the Capena Gate. The noise was deafening. Jesus had never heard such horrendous sounds, not even in Jerusalem on the great holy days. No one seemed to talk; everyone was yelling. It was a babble of tongues in languages Jesus had never before heard. Ruf pointed out a group of slaves from Gaul, a pair of swarthy merchants from Syria, a handful of handsome, black Carthagenians from northern Africa, and a group of young men like themselves whom Ruf said were students from Spain.

Jesus knew the sun had not yet set but felt boxed in, almost suffocated, in these narrow streets whose tall buildings blocked out the light. And everyone was in a hurry. People rushing this way, running that way, bumping carelessly into one another, men pushing carts headlong into passing groups—all created the impression of chaos. Urban was leading the group along the Appian Road but skirted the Circus Maximus through side streets and lanes, following along the foot of the Aventine hill down to the Tiber River. He was anxious to arrive at his home located in the commercial district facing the river.

Darkness was beginning to fall upon the streets. Shopkeepers were carrying their wares off the streets into their shops, some locking doors and others closing iron gates. Here and there torches were being lighted on the outside walls of cafes. The group was now alongside the Tiber. Jesus did not like the river with the muddy, brown color, strewn with refuse and loaded with the traffic of barges and small boats. He longed for the crystal clear water of the streams and rivers of Galilee.

"Hey! Hey!" Urban let out a long, loud yell. "Come, Martinus. Come, Decius."

The servants came running toward them. They took charge of the wagon, took the parcels Urban, Joseph, and Simon were handing them, and respectfully extended welcomes. They ushered the group down the street to the building where four torches lighted up the entrance to Urban's store.

The travelers entered through the center door whose iron hinges were fastened to the side of an arch made of tufa stone. Inside, the oblong, spacious room looked like a combination small warehouse and store which, in fact, it was. It gave the appearance of being a long cave with merchandise hung haphazardly on the walls and spilling over the long tables that formed four rows as far back as the eye could see. Obviously, Urban was operating a successful mercantile business as well as being Joseph's agent.

Urban led the group past rows of merchandise similar to the cargo the *Jubilee* had carried from Caesarea to Puteoli. In the rear of the building he directed them to a stairway and urged them to ascend as he himself followed behind them. Joseph led the group.

"Be careful of the step above the landing, Joseph," Urban cried from the rear. "I still have not had the time to repair it."

"Urban," Joseph shouted back, "you said that last year and the year before."

"You remember, Joseph, Rome is eternal. Things move slowly, very slowly, here."

"And that, Urban, I heard many times before." Both laughed.

The travelers stood in the entrance of a spacious, second-story room, tastefully appointed with huge tapestries with scenes of meadows, rivers, pastures, and cozy farmhouses. The room was softly lighted by torches extending from the four walls. Between the torches were doors, at least twenty of them, leading into parlors, bedrooms, and kitchens. A large table, covered with a white linen tablecloth and vases of bright flowers, stood in the center of the room.

At the end of the room stood five young men; two were black and three were fair-skinned; no doubt, thought Jesus, slaves that Urban had purchased. In the center of the room stood two women and two children. Urban hastened to the women and children with Joseph and Alexander following in his steps. Simon, Ari, and Jesus fell in line.

"My dear," said Urban. He brushed a kiss on the lips of a young matron who appeared to be ten years his junior. "I am glad you have everything ready for our guests."

"Urban, we have not been married these ten years without knowing you honor our house by your safe return and the company of your friends." She turned to the group behind her husband. "Shalom! Blessed be God!"

Joseph approached and embraced her. "Shalom! Antonia. We are greateful again for your gracious hospitality. I trust we will not be too great a burden on you and your household in the coming days. You know, of course, our good captain, Alexander."

"Welcome, welcome indeed," Antonia replied. By this time Urban had dispatched servants to attend to the luggage and place it in the guests' rooms.

"Forgive me!" Antonia exclaimed. "Urban has been so busy with his homecoming that I have neglected my duties. Permit me. This is my cousin, Julia, and you know, of course, our children Hermes and Olympas." Joseph bowed to Julia and patted the children on their heads.

"These, Antonia," Joseph replied, motioning the others to come forward, "are my good friends. Aristarchus from Thessalonica is Captain Alexander's first mate. Simon, our faithful cook, is the father of Ruf and Alex whom you have befriended. And this is Jesus, son of Joseph of Nazareth, in the remote country of Galilee."

The two groups exchanged greetings and pleasantries. When Jesus approached Julia, he greeted her with "Shalom!" She returned the same greeting.

"I am surprised," said Jesus, "that you greet me as a Jew. I deeply appreciate your thoughtfulness."

"Do not be surprised, Jesus," Julia replied with a hint of laughter in her voice. "I am like Urban and Antonia. We believe in Yahweh and strive to follow the Law. I also study the sacred writings and sing your sacred songs."

"Then doubly must I express my gratitude to you, Julia."

"And what do you mean by that, Jesus?"

"I am indebted to you for the toga that you have made for me. I already tried it on, with the help of Ruf. It is finely woven and matches the tunic my mother had woven for me for this journey. I must confess, though, I cannot understand why you should favor me so when we had not even met."

"And that, Jesus, may be simply because as we both know, God's ways are not man's ways. Now what was your other reason for appreciation?"

"I am grateful, Julia," Jesus replied with a seriousness in his voice that Julia immediately felt, "because you are a

God-fearing Gentile. I know that Yahweh has destined you to be a good friend of mine. For that I thank you and Yahweh."

Julia was amazed by the directness and seriousness of this young man. She did, however, recall Urban saying that Joseph of Arimathea was bringing along on the journey a most unusual young man. Most unusual, indeed, she thought.

"I will need your help, Julia."

"I beg your pardon, Jesus." Julia noticed that the others in the group had scattered and the servants were busy carrying out their assigned duties. She and Jesus were standing quite alone in the center of the room.

"I will need your help in the days to come," Jesus repeated. He smiled reassuringly, a smile of a man at least twice his age who appeared in complete control of any eventuality. "After all, Julia, you made this beautiful toga for me. Now you must help in seeing that I know when to wear it."

Julia was flustered. She did not know what to say. She was at least five years older than her new friend, yet she was drawn to him, attracted with a serene love she had never before felt.

"Julia!" The voice was Antonia's. "Come, now, and help us serve our guests."

"Jesus!" The voice was Alex's. "Come. We must wash for dinner."

"Do not be afraid, Julia." Jesus spoke softly and touched her hand. "What will be, will be God's will."

Julia smiled, touched his hand, and replied, "I am not afraid." She turned and went to help her cousin.

* * * * * *

The following days were a travelogue of Rome for Jesus. Urban assigned Ruf and Alex the task of showing the young man from Galilee all the marvels and wonders of this center of the world.

"Do not leave him out of your sight," cautioned Joseph the merchant. "I cannot go back home without him."

Urban turned to Ruf and Alex. "Your job depends on this," he spoke softly but firmly. No further words were needed.

The three young men left Urban's establishment exhilarated each day. Some days Simon accompanied them; other times Ari joined them. On the days Simon joined them, they were like father and three sons; when Ari came along they were like four brothers. The days they were on their own they were like schoolboys on the first day of vacation.

At times Ari had a difficult time asserting his seniority. Ruf or Alex would gently and jokingly remind him that he was not here the first mate of the *Jubilee*. He acquiesced with mock seriousness. On these days Ari watched Jesus as closely as a leopard his jungle prey. He recalled their conversation at the inn near Three Taverns; as a matter of fact, he recalled it several times each day. He planned to talk about this great Yahweh with Elaina when he returned to Thessalonica.

One day the threesome, without Simon or Ari, crossed the dirty, muddy Tiber on one of the crowded, clamorous, pushing-and-shoving barges the city fathers offered as public transportation. They heaved a sigh of relief when they left the river behind them and had passed through that area across the Tiber that deserved to be called "a den of iniquity." They climbed the hairpin curves of the hillside called the Janiculum with a speed not even excelled by the army's crack alpine corps.

Jesus said he wanted to see the temple dedicated to Janus

whom the Romans called the god of doorways because he had two faces, one facing east and the other west. Of course, Jesus did not believe that, nor did many Romans. He had heard on the *Jubilee* that the temple had a double gate that was open during wartime to allow the Roman army to march in and out of the city in the terrible business of making war. He also heard that these gates were closed in times of peace, which happened only four times as far back as people could remember. One of those times was shortly before he was born, when Augustus proclaimed the empire was at peace. He told Ruf and Alex these things as they approached the temple.

"I am glad," said Jesus, "that the gates of this temple are closed. It shows that even pagan people who do not know Yahweh are dedicated to peace."

"The Romans have a saying," Alex said, "that my teachers said came from their famous orator, Cicero."

"And the saying?"

"If you want peace, prepare for war."

"But is it true?" Jesus replied. "To me preparing for war is the first step in waging war."

Another day the three with Ari set out to explore the theater of Marcellus and the coliseum. Another day... And another day... Jesus continually marveled at the sights of this fabulous city. He reflected on the ingenuity of the human mind in creating so great a center of government, commerce, art, and architecture. Most of the latter, Ari reminded him, was stolen from Greece.

One day, returning to Urban's house, the three young men found themselves in an area Jesus had not seen before.

"Where are we?" he asked Alex.

"We are not far from Urban's house. Hurry now." Alex hesitated telling Jesus that they were in an area regarded as off limits to most people. He did not want to admit that they were on Palatine Hill, the home of the emperor, his family, and other royal favorites. Inadvertently they had passed the street at the foot of the hill that would lead them to Urban's home.

"But, Alex," Jesus said, slackening his pace.

"Hurry!" said Alex, and as he quickened his pace, so did Ruf.

"Honestly, where are we?" Jesus asked, purposely lagging behind the two.

"Come along, Jesus. Hurry! We are now on Palatine

Hill. Jesus, run. Quick!"

Alex was not just frightened; he was terrified. What would Simon say? What would Joseph think? What would his future be with Urban? He glanced over his shoulder and saw Jesus and Ruf running behind him. He saw the street leading to the Circus Maximus in the distance. With a gasp he noticed the Praetorian guards at the foot of the hill, guarding the entrance to the boulevard. No other traffic or people were on the boulevard. He turned and placed his arms around Jesus and Ruf. He hoped the guards would think them to be only misdirected visitors on a lark. Alex prayed; so did Ruf and Jesus. They passed the guards with no questions asked. Alex heaved a sigh of relief. They were back again in safety on the banks of the Tiber. Urban's store was in sight.

"I am glad," said Jesus to Alex, "that you showed me the palace of Augustus."

"I did not mean to, Jesus. Please, do not tell anyone we were on the Palatine Hill."

"I will not. But thanks, again."

* * * * * *

The three young men had washed and dressed for dinner. They entered the large dining room, took their places, and were soon joined by Simon and Ari. Urban, Joseph, Alexander, and Antonia were seated in the center of the table. Julia took her place beside Antonia.

"Now, Jesus," Joseph was in one of his expansive moods, "have you seen enough of Rome?"

"I have, Joseph. Alex and Ruf were expert guides. I hope that Urban keeps them as his apprentices."

"I shall, indeed," said Urban. He beckoned to the servants to pour the wine.

"Now for the good news," said Joseph.

"Hear! Hear!" Everyone around the table knew what the good news would be but wanted Joseph to have the satisfaction of telling it.

"Tomorrow we begin our journey home!"

"Thank the gods," said Alexander. Everyone knew he was tired of the city and eager to get back on the deck of the *Jubilee*.

"We have spent a good week in Rome," said Joseph, politely ignoring the captain. "Thanks to Urban, we have sold our merchandise at a good profit and have another full cargo to take back to Caesarea. In your name I thank Urban, his charming wife, Antonia, and Julia for their gracious hospitality."

The guests pounded their approval with their fists on the table. "Our faithful Simon," Joseph continued, "will return home to Cyrene before we come again to Rome. By the time we return, he hopes to see his sons as doctors of the law."

Simon smiled proudly. Ruf and Alex looked puzzled, for Joseph did not know it would be four more years before they could be lawyers.

"I cannot wait until I plant my feet on the boards of the *Jubilee*," said Alexander. Everyone knew that already and laughed. Again all pounded their approval on the top of the table.

"Good," said Joseph. "Now eat and drink and bless Yahweh for the success he has given our venture."

"Praise God!" The cry went up from those around the table and even Ari uttered the prayer.

Jesus sat in silent thought, unnoticed by his companions. The festivities of the evening were marred by a note of sadness on the part of Simon and his sons. They would not see each other for another year at least. The boys knew the sacrifices their father was making to keep them in school.

"Thank the gods," Ari exclaimed, breaking the silence of

the little group. "We are getting out of this city of beggars and thieves and politicians even worse than the thieves. With due respect, Jesus, I also thank your great Yahweh!"

Jesus smiled but remained deep in his own thoughts. Time was running out and he had not yet accomplished his mission. He quickly reviewed in his mind the route Alex, Ruf, and he had taken that afternoon from the Palatine Hill. He knew he could find his way, even if the streets were dimly lit. But how would he pass the guards? A person would have to be a magician. He was definitely not a magician.

As the wine poured more freely, the conversation became louder and happier. Urban was again the gracious host in his own home. He had gifts for everyone and an appropriate remark for each of his friends. Joseph received a fine calfskin parchment with a map of the world elegantly painted on it in golden ink. Captain Alexander received a similar parchment, only his contained a map of the constellations of the stars.

Urban approached the section of the table where Jesus sat. His arms were laden with gifts. He offered Simon a box containing a carving knife, fork, and spoon made of sterling silver with ebony handles. "These," he said as he set the box before Simon, "are not for your galley aboard the *Jubilee*. They are meant for your good wife, Esther, when you return to Cyrene." Simon thanked his host profusely.

"Ari, Captain Alexander told me of the young lady who waits for you in Thessalonica." Urban set before him a small case coverd with white watered silk. "Do not worry," Urban continued, "I am confident she waits for you because I know she could not find a better man." Ari opened the case and gazed at a string of pearls. "The pearls come from the waters that lap the shores of distant India," Urban added as Ari rose and embraced him. Jesus saw tears welling up in the first mate's eyes.

"For you, Jesus, I have a very small and different gift. I do not know quite what it means or how you will use it, but my men searched through many warehouses along the Tiber and finally found this." Urban set a small leather box before him. Jesus opened it, gently and slowly. He looked down on a small golden triangle with no decorations, no engravings.

From my heart, Urban, I thank you. Do you know why you chose this beautiful triangle?"

"For the life of me," said Urban, "I do not. Captain Alexander told me that you were fascinated by the triangle that rests atop the prow of Joseph's ship. This, I thought, might be the best reminder of your journey to Rome."

"Thank you again, Urban. You may never know how I might use this gift. Some day, I hope you will come to know the full meaning of this symbol." Urban was puzzled by the remark. He asked no question but moved on with his gifts to the others.

Jesus returned to the land of his own thoughts, a stranger to the world of laughter, merriment, good cheer, and conversation surrounding him. He held the golden triangle in his hand, glancing at it from time to time. The sands in the hourglass of his own plan were running thin.

His eyes fell upon Julia, seated next to Antonia. He studied her features more carefully. She wore an ankle-length dress of saffron color that fell in graceful folds from her shoulders. Her complexion was of a whiteness uncommon among his own people and reminded him of the snows atop Mount Hebron. Her brown eyes accentuated auburn hair that fell loosely over her shoulders. Her small, oval face reflected an inner steadiness and calmness.

Why had Julia spent so much time and effort in making so handsome a toga for him? She certainly had a reason, perhaps a reason that even she did not know. Jesus excused himself and told his friends he wanted to speak with Julia. He crossed the room, approached her and asked if he might speak with her alone. She rose and the two withdrew to a corner of the room.

"Julia," Jesus began, "I have been puzzled these days why you should make so beautiful a toga for me. Did you have a reason?"

"My friend," Julia replied softly and looked directly into his eyes, "I heard from Urban that you hope to meet the great Augustus. He has demanded that the toga be worn by Romans. I thought you would be dressed better as a Roman gentleman than a Galilean carpenter." She smiled. Jesus was moved by her directness in speech.

"How will I ever wear it," Jesus continued, "when we leave at dawn? It was kind and thoughtful of you, Julia, but I fear..."

"Do not fear, Jesus. If you wish to see the emperor, you shall. Please ask no more questions." Julia's tone showed that she was in full command of the situation. "Dress yourself in your finest clothes—the tunic your mother made for you and over it, the toga I wove for you. Meet me in front of the store in five minutes. Go quickly and quietly and speak to no one."

8

The Palace of the Emperor

Julia stood in the shadows of the entrance to Urban's store. She had thrown a large brown cloak over her dinner dress and the attached hood covered herhead. Jesus approached wearing the tunic his mother wove, with the purple trimming showing through about his knees. He had Julia's toga draped above his body and its folds wrapped awkwardly in his elbows. He had on his feet the new sandals his uncle, Cleophas, had made for him. Julia surveyed him with a glance and thought he might not look like a Roman but he was surely one of the best dressed and finest looking young men she had ever seen.

Together they moved hurriedly away from Urban's

store. Julia took a torch from the folds of her cloak and lighted it from a torch fastened to the wall at the corner.

"Now tell me, please, Julia, how you plan this meeting with the mighty Augustus?"

"I have not planned your meeting with him, Jesus, but I know how you can pass the guards."

"How will we accomplish that?"

Julia blushed, but Jesus could not see her complexion change to crimson. "I have a friend," she continued, "a very good and dear friend. He is the captain of the Praetorian Guards. I know he is the officer on duty tonight. I have spoken to him about you and he said he would help."

"He must be a very close friend, Julia, to be willing to do so much for a person he does not know."

"He is, Jesus. I love him very much. But he is still a pagan and does not believe in our great Yahweh nor does he follow the Law. But he is a good man, Jesus, and if he comes to believe, I hope and pray that we will marry."

"What is the captain's name, Julia?" Jesus was walking slightly behind her as they picked their way cautiously through the rubble and refuse that cluttered the street at night.

"His name is Longinus. His father was a soldier in Caesar's army during the campaigns in Gaul. His mother was a captive from Britain but Longinus cannot remember her. He has spent his whole life in the army and must be a very good soldier because he was chosen as a captain in the Praetorian guards. You must pray, Jesus, that he will come to share our faith in Yahweh."

"I am sure Longinus will come to share our faith."

The street had widened into a boulevard by now and Jesus knew they were climbing the Palatine Hill. On his right he saw the lights shining from almost every room in the palace of the Empress Livia. From the gardens surrounding her palace he heard music and laughter. He and Julia were passing along a wall which he judged must be at least ten feet tall. Within he heard the splashing of water in the fountains, but no other sounds, and he smelled the sweet scent of magnolia trees in full bloom. The building enclosed was dimly lit except for an apartment in the northwest corner. The lights seemed to come from the second floor of an otherwise seemingly deserted building.

"Here," said Julia, speaking very softly, "is the palace of Augustus. The light you see above is from his study. The lights you see ahead are the gates of the palace. There we shall meet Longinus."

"Halt! Who goes there?" The harsh, commanding voice shattered the stillness of the night. A young man, perhaps a dozen years older than Jesus, approached in full military armor. The light from Julia's torch reflected on his breastplate.

"It is Julia." The soldier approached less cautiously and more relaxed.

"It is good to see you, my dear." He bent over and lightly kissed her. "I had thought you might not be coming, for it is getting late."

"This, Longinus, is our young friend, Jesus of Galilee."

"I am happy to meet you. Julia has told me much about you and your strange insistence on seeing the emperor." Longinus gave a curt military nod whose casualness betrayed the warmth of his own feelings. "I see you are dressed for the occasion." Longinus laughed, for he knew Julia wove the toga, and Jesus and Julia joined in his laughter. "It is a strange request you have made, Jesus."

"I know Longinus, but it is a most important one. The emperor of this small world must come at least to know the Ruler of the universe. That is why I must see him."

"Those words, you know, could be interpreted as treason. But from Julia I have heard about your Yahweh and know they are not."

"I am grateful to you, Longinus, for the risk you are taking."

"And you, my friend, are about to take a greater risk. Well might the emperor command me to seize you and throw you into the Mamertine Prison."

"I am prepared for that risk, Longinus."

"Let us be quick, then. Julia, you best return to Urban's home. If all goes well, I will escort Jesus back there myself. If things do not go well, then—then you best pray to your Yahweh." Longinus stooped and kissed Julia again. Quickly she departed.

"Come. Walk softly and do not speak. Follow me." Longinus turned to Jesus, turned again, and walked toward the huge iron gates of the palace. Jesus followed closely behind.

Longinus saluted the corporal at the gate, said nothing, and led Jesus into the gardens. They passed through the ornate entrance of the palace, down one long corridor, up a flight of marble stairs, turned left, and headed in the direction of a light shining through two heavy damask drapes.

"I can lead you no further, my friend. I will be at the gate if I am not commanded to seize you before you are finished." Longinus turned quickly and walked quietly away. Jesus stood momentarily, offered a prayer to Yahweh and walked in the direction of the room.

"My Lord," Jesus said. He parted the curtains and made a deep, revential bow. "My name is Jesus of Galilee and I am one of your subjects." He stood motionless, his body clothed in the white toga, appearing almost as a vision in front of the deep red drapes.

"Who? What? Get out! Get out!" Augustus stammered from behind the writing desk where he was standing. "Get out! How dare you!" Several papers fell from the desk as he pounded it with both his fists.

"My Lord," Jesus said again, not making a single movement. "I have come as your loyal subject to talk with you about peace. I beg you in the name of my great God, Yahweh, to receive me." Again Jesus bowed deeply, his hands on his knees and his head almost reaching his knees.

"Outrage! Out! Guards! Guards!" Augustus shouted at least ten times louder than he usually did.

No sounds of marching feet in the corridor. No movement except the papers the emperor nervously and angrily shuffled on his desk. A handful of moments seemed eternity. Jesus stood motionless. Augustus made the first move.

He emerged from the light descending over his desk and shuffled toward his young intruder. Jesus noted that he dragged his left foot slightly behind his right as he walked. The emperor looked many years older than Urban's report indicated. His left eye was partially closed and twitched irregularly. His complexion was sallow, no doubt accentuated by the unruly yellow hair that fell helter-skelter around his ears and over his brow.

Jesus moved forward slowly, approached the old man, bent his knee and reached to kiss the emperor's hand. "My Lord, I have traveled many miles to bring you the gift of peace. I pray that the peace of Yahweh be with you and in you. In my native tongue that means 'Shalom.'"

Augustus looked down upon this youth kneeling before him. Many years had passed since any of his subjects, except his beloved wife, ever came so close to him. He could not remember when anyone was ever so bold as to come into his presence unannounced and unwanted. Only Agrippa and Maecenas ever spoke so calmly and directly to him. Perhaps, yes, this young man reminded him of Agrippa, his closest friend. But the snow of the Appenines had melted five times since he himself had buried Agrippa. This youth was no ghost. The thought of Agrippa softened his heart.

"Rise. Do not grovel before me for you will receive no benefit except that I may spare your life." Jesus noted a softening in the tone of the voice. He rose and looked directly into the dim and glassy eyes of this man who had in his quaking voice more power than any human being. Augustus stepped closer to him, examining him from top to bottom, walking around him, and as a man accustomed to making quick decisions, looked into Jesus' eyes and said, "You are no assassin. You may be a fool, but my empire is full of fools. Tell me who you are."

Without flinching and with a sturdiness in his voice that disarmed the emperor, Jesus replied, "I am Jesus, son of Joseph, the carpenter in Nazareth of Galilee. For many weeks I have traveled with Joseph, the merchant of Arimathea in Judea, to see you, my Lord, and speak with you of peace."

"Do you not see I am too busy, too burdened, with all these affairs of state? How can I have time, even if I wanted it, to talk to any and every subject who wants to talk to me?"

"The answer, my Lord, is simple. Take time."

The emperor liked that remark. Often he had posed the same question to scores of philosophers and counselsors and they gave him nothing but studies, surveys, and platitudes. Some even tried to explain that he could make more hours in the day. Nonsense!

"Take time!" The old man chuckled to himself. "I suppose in the end that is the best way to live. I once heard a singer—not a very good one—sing something about taking one day at a time. Yes, young man, take time. I cannot remember talking with anyone so young as you since my stepsons Gaius and Drusus died. What a loss! I had hoped one or the other would have been my successor. Well, now, let us take time."

The emperor turned and shuffled off, taking tiny steps in an uncertain manner as many old men do. He motioned Jesus to follow and indicated that he should sit beside him on the couch next to his working desk.

Jesus glanced about the room. It was practically bare except for the working desk, the couch, and a long table in a dim corner whose top was covered with papers. The emperor obviously did not delegate very much of his work. Urban was correct; this emperor studied every detail, explored every approach, before arriving at a decision.

"Now, my rude intruder," the emperor was speaking

the words with a touch of warmth in his voice, "if we are going to talk, we must have wine. There, over there on the table someplace, is a decanter full of wine and some glasses. The servants bring it in every evening and take it out every morning, untouched. I cannot work when drinking wine. But they do it and I say nothing. Did you ever think the emperor might be no more than a slave to his own slaves? Never mind. They say wine is the elixir of the gods, and they tell me I am a god."

Jesus turned midway between the couch and the table. "But, my Lord, you know you are not a god."

"I know. I know."

Jesus walked to the table, filled two goblets with wine and returned to the couch, offering one to the emperor. "Begging your pardon, my Lord, you seem to make the empire your god."

"It is. It is. Young man, I have spent these fifty-two years in bringing order out of chaos. The empire is my life and my life is the empire. How else could I govern, how else unite so many different people in so vast an area, than place one god supreme over all their petty, jealous gods? That god is the Genius of Rome and in my person I embody that genius."

"Your genius no one doubts, my Lord. But to make a god out of the state, to make the state the purpose of every citizen's life is—and I beg your pardon for saying it—idolatry. There is only one God, my Lord, and I believe that you yourself know this God is above even you and the empire. That God I call Yahweh who governs not only princes and states and even the emperor but every one of the little people who live in this vast empire."

The emperor looked intently at his young guest. He admired both his courage and wisdom. He wondered which he admired more. He shifted the weight of his weary, fragile body from one side to the other. Details... Agrippa always said his genius was in his command of details.

"Tell me again, young man, your name and where you are from."

"I am called Jesus of Nazareth in Galilee. They call Joseph the carpenter my father and my mother is Mary, daughter of Joachim and Anne. We are, my Lord, descendants of our great King David."

"Ah! Then you are ambitious. You are seeking a favor."

"None, my Lord. I seek only the favor of Yahweh."

"How old are you, young man?"

"Fourteen, soon to be fifteen."

"Then you were born during the reign of King Herod. Tell me, in your country do they call him Herod the Great?"

"Some people may, my Lord, but not those who are faithful to the faith of my ancestors. I have heard that you often overlooked his treacheries and atrocities."

"That is true, I fear. Perhaps I overlooked too much. But he paid the tribute and kept many of the rebels in your land under control. An emperor cannot be responsible for all the deeds his underlings commit. Or, would you disagree with that?"

"I would, my Lord." Jesus hesitated a moment, then continued, "An emperor might not know everything his representatives do, but when he knows, and knows for certain, what they do is wrong, he must remove them, for then he is responsible.

"I have tried to do that, young man. But even an emperor cannot know everything and be responsible for everything."

"That, my Lord, is why there must be one supreme God who will set the scales of justice right, rewarding the good and punishing the evil."

"You would say, then, that the murder of those baby boys in Bethlehem fourteen years ago was a crime?"

"I would, my Lord."

"But in his report, as I recall it, Herod said there was evidence that a new king was born in Bethlehem. He said wise men from far distant countries came seeking this newborn king whose star of his birth they had been following. Herod said he was forced to kill all the baby boys lest there be a rebellion against the empire. You know your country is always on the verge of rebellion."

"That, my Lord, was his report. He knew nothing of the prophecies of my people concerning such a king. He feared only for his own power. I have often heard the story from my own parents and relatives. You see, my Lord, I was born in Bethlehem. My parents were there to be enrolled in the census you decreed. I was fortunate, for my parents took me and fled into Egypt. That way my life was spared. Not even the tyranny of men can thwart the design of God."

The emperor leaned closer and looked searchingly into the face of Jesus. "You mean, young man, that you were one who escaped from Herod's massacre? Unbelievable!" The emperor sipped from his goblet. He was thinking, recalling events from the past. A deadening stillness fell upon the room. Not even the noise of Rome penetrated the windows of this room that looked more like the cell of an Essene than the palace of the ruler of the world.

"It should not be so incomprehensible, my Lord. Our sacred writers frequently remind us that God's ways are not man's ways nor are his thoughts man's thoughts. If you cannot believe, can you at least recognize that an Almighty God intervenes in the affairs of men?"

"Our poets have also written such thoughts." The emperor was speaking slowly, thoughtfully, almost to himself. "One says we have entered a golden age, that the earth will blossom forth and the son of a god will appear among us and he will rule mightily and the gift he will bring is peace. Virgil wrote that; did you know that?"

"No, my Lord." A silence fell between them during which the one was thinking and the other was praying.

"Virgil was a flatterer, you know." The emperor cleared his throat. "He expected me to believe those words applied to me. I am not so old a man, young man, as to forget my origins and know my limitations. The older I get the more I have a genuine fear of the god I do not know but do know must exist."

"That fear, my Lord, is what one of our sacred writers calls the beginning of wisdom."

"One thing I know, or perhaps it is just a feeling, perhaps a premonition. As I read the reports that cross my desk from every corner of the empire, I sense that our world is standing on the edge of a new, a marvelous age. I have tried to put my finger on what it might be, but somehow the reasons escape me, even though the feeling remains. I often sense a desire, a deep-seated, almost desperate, longing among millions of people for a noble purpose in life, a reason that makes sense out of life and living."

The old man paused, squinted into the light surrounding his work bench. He seemed to be in a distant world all his own. Jesus studied his face more carefully. It was an old face, wrinkled like dried leather. His eyes, gazing into the light, revealed a weariness of soul and hunger of heart that seemed to border on despair. Jesus felt sorry for him. The two sat in silence. Only the water splashing in the fountains below could be heard.

"Where was I? Oh yes, this new golden age that Virgil and Maecenas so much like to write and talk about." The emperor rose and started shuffling back and forth in front of Jesus. "They are all gone now, and after Agrippa, I miss Maecenas the most. He was a genius like Agrippa, you know. They were the only ones I could really trust besides the Empress Livia. She has always been my most intimate counselor."

"Our wise men tell us," Jesus added gently, "a man is blessed beyond all wealth who has a good and faithful wife."

"It was she, you know—but how could you know?" The emperor stood in his tracks, paused a moment, then continued, "She more than anyone encouraged me to bring peace to all corners of the empire."

"My Lord, I was born during the time of this peace. Even scholars in my own small country speak of the whole world being at peace because of your rule. For that I am grateful. You have succeeded—to a point."

Augustus turned on his heels. "And what, young man, do you mean by 'to a point'? I think it rather impudent that a country boy like you should lecture the ruler of the world." The emperor gathered the folds of his toga in his arms and sat on the edge of the couch. "Now, tell me more."

"My Lord, I mean no disrespect. Your accomplishment has been great and no one doubts the benefits the whole empire has enjoyed by the Peace of Rome. Permit me, with due respect, merely to suggest that the golden age you dream of, the new era and the new world you sense is in the dawning, can never be realized by a peace built on fear. The peace the empire enjoys is tenuous. It is not a full and honest peace. Do I dare go on?"

"Go on. Go on. You speak with a wisdom far beyond your years."

"The Peace of Rome, the *Pax Romana*, is expressed in the words of one of your own senators; I believe he was Cicero. He said that if you want peace, you must prepare for war. That, as I see it and many of the sacred writers of my people see it, is only a shadow of real peace. Some, I know, will say that you must have a vast army and a mighty navy to maintain this peace. I think such might and force instills fear into the hearts of people and they come to think of themselves as living under an unbearable bondage and burden of taxes."

Jesus paused. The emperor turned so that their glances met. He searched the eyes of the young man. "You have spoken wisely, but I do not think you fully realize the difficulties of government. I do not believe that might makes right, but I do believe and so have governed that power is indispensable in preserving law and order."

"That, my Lord, is the genius of the Peace of Rome. It has served you well enough, indeed. But it did not go far enough, nor deep enough. Law and order is but one aspect of peace. Often it is maintained only by fear. Fear will never bring about the golden age. Only love, my Lord, only love is the solid fountain of true peace. That is the *Pax Christi*—the Peace of the Anointed One."

"But this *Pax Christi*—this Peace of the Anointed One—is but a longing in the hearts of men for a kingdom of justice and love and peace. Imagination! Pure imagination!"

"I do not think so, my Lord. You dream of a golden age and your poets sing about it. There will be no new age or new world until 'the Anointed One' appears and people follow his teachings. He seeks no great empire such as yours, only the love of human beings for one another. That is all he desires. That, my Lord, is why one of our sacred writers has called him 'the Prince of Peace.'"

"I have often dreamed of these things, but knew they were no more than dreams. How I wish there would be people of love in an empire of peace! But, then, this 'Anointed One' who is to bring his peace, must be chosen, anointed, set apart by someone. He must be commissioned, must he not?"

"Indeed, my Lord. His other name given by our prophets is 'Emmanuel,' which means 'God-with-us.' Even your own Virgil, as you said, in some strange prophetic words announced that a virgin would bring forth a child and through that child the world would blossom forth with peace."

The emperor rose, and as he did, so did Jesus. The emperor paced back and forth across the floor. Jesus stood in silence beside the couch.

"You say, Jesus, this 'Anointed One' would be 'God-with-us.' Do you mean that this God would come to earth and seize all empires and kingdoms?"

"Not in the way you are thinking, my Lord. The 'Anointed One' comes as God among his people, like his people. He desires no worldly kingdom or power. His rule is one of love found in the hearts of those who follow him and adore him. You need not fear such a kingdom, my Lord. The 'Anointed One' will lift up these people, carry their burdens, be one with them and call them his brothers and sisters."

"Such a one, " the emperor said thoughtfully, "such a person would cause a revolution."

"He will indeed, my Lord. That will then be the dawning of the new era and new world you dream about. Birth causes pain but also gives life."

"You come speaking words of peace with an otherwordly wisdom about peace," the emperor said slowly. "You have given me much to think about. But now I must return to work. What is your name?"

"Jesus of Nazareth."

"Go, Jesus; return to Nazareth."

"My Lord," said Jesus as he reached into the pocket of his tunic, "I have a small gift to give you because you have been a gift to millions who do not even know you."

"A gift?" The emperor was stammering. "You, Jesus, you have given me much already."

"This gift is a symbol of a greater gift, a greater mystery, than even you in all your power will not live to see unfold."

Jesus reached for the emperor's hand. He opened the weather-beaten, deeply veined hand and placed within its palm a small gold triangle. The emperor stared at it blankly, almost blindly.

"My Lord," Jesus continued, "you recognize a Supreme God above all other gods, even the god of the empire. That God is Yahweh, the God of my fathers. You will not live to see, my Lord, but other emperors on your throne will come to know and worship the one true God. The God who is Father. The God who is Son. The God who is Holy Spirit. This God is Three-in-One. Treasure this golden triangle and pray to this God who is Three-in-One. He is Emmanuel: God-with-us."

Jesus rose, turned slowly and walked to the door. The emperor sat bewildered. At the doorway Jesus turned, raised his right hand, and said, "The Lord bless you and keep you! The Lord let his face shine upon you, and be gracious to you! The Lord look upon you kindly and give you peace."

Jesus walked slowly down the corridor and staircase, passed the guards unnoticed and entered the wide boulevard. From the shadow of one of the bushes a figure approached.

"Do not be afraid. It is Longinus." Jesus greeted him with a warm embrace and thanked him for his help. "I waited to guide you back to Urban's house lest you forgot the way."

"I am grateful to you, Longinus. No words can tell how grateful." The two walked together in silence. Longinus asked no questions. In his mind he thought over and over how strange it was that a young man from such a distant country should appear before the emperor, visit with him so long and depart unnoticed and unharmed. This Jesus was, indeed, a most exceptional young man.

They climbed the stairs of Urban's house and before they reached the door, Urban opened it. Jesus walked over directly to Joseph and Longinus approached Julia. Joseph rose.

"Shalom!" said Jesus.

"Shalom!" Joseph replied. They embraced warmly, Joseph holding Jesus firmly in his arms.

"I have seen the emperor."

"I know," said Joseph. "Praise the Lord!"

"Praise the Lord!" said Jesus.

9
The Return Voyage

On a brilliant and bright morning when the Tyrennean Sea matched the blue of the sky, the *Jubilee* edged its way out of the harbor of Puteoli. Captain Alexander was in his expansive mood, obviously happy to be master in his own domain again. Joseph was content with the completion of his successful business transactions and had renewed confidence in the financial acumen of Urban. Nick was pleased with himself, knowing that he had performed his duties well. Ari stood on the deck issuing orders to the sailors who were laboriously rowing the *Jubilee* through the jigsaw puzzle of the harbor. Simon and Jesus were in the galley, preparing the noonday meal.

Jesus spoke only to Joseph and Ari about his visit with the emperor. He did not, of course, tell them everything the two discussed. He did not feel that even such close friends needed to know everything that he and the mighty ruler of the empire talked about.

The return voyage of the *Jubilee* was uneventful. The ship retraced the course it followed on its journey to Rome. Jesus was pleased when Ari joined Nick and him to visit the venerable old rabbi and synagogue in Myra. Jesus laughed with Ari when they heard the booming and boisterous shouts of Barnabas when he boarded the ship in Seleucia. Jesus was sad when he bade farewell to Captain Alexander, Simon, Ari, and the other sailors on the pier in Caesarea. Philip, the harbor master, was his usual meticulous and officious self. He commented to Joseph that the young man from Nazareth seemed to have matured a great deal during the voyage. Nick rented a wagon and two burros in Herod's city for the return journey to Nazareth, Jerusalem, and Arimathea. Joseph and Nick took Jesus home to his parents.

Home... Jesus was content to be back to his mother's kitchen and Joseph's carpenter shop. He spoke of his journey to his cousins, Simon and Jude, his uncle, Cleophas, his other friends, neighbors, and parents. Only to his parents, though, did Jesus speak of his meeting with Augustus. Joseph and Mary listened with awe and amazement, not fully comprehending what their son meant by all the words in his conversation with the emperor.

In time Jesus' journey to Rome was forgotten by the citizens of Nazareth. All but one. Mary frequently pondered in the silence of her own heart the strange words Jesus had with Augustus. Joseph died and Jesus became the sole support of his mother, Mary. He was called by family, friends, and neighbors "the son of Joseph the Carpenter."

* * * * * *

The emperor grew older. Some intimates said he became most irritated when people called him Augustus. He lost his interest in the affairs of government. State documents laid on his desk week after week. Politcal observers and stockbrokers said Tiberias, not Octavian, now ruled the empire.

Not a day passed without the old man recalling his visit with Jesus, the son of a carpenter. He spoke not a word about that night, not even to Livia. But he wondered day after day what the young man from Nazareth was doing. He knew better than to make inquiries through official channels, even though he was often tempted to do so. He asked himself how Jesus would bring about his kingdom of love and justice and peace in a new age. He longed to talk with him again! He had so many questions to ask.

He became more of a recluse, more concerned with his own thoughts than a war along the Danube or an uprising among the Parthians. He had tried to deal so often for so many years with such problems. How would the Anointed One deal with them?

What was this mystery he uttered that night about a God who is Three-in-One? How could this God Three-in-One be the God-with-us?

Not a day passed that he did not take the golden triangle from his pocket and finger it slowly, tenderly, in the palm of his hand. The empress often noticed it but said nothing.

He was again Octavian, not Augustus. He smiled when he thought of the days when people hailed him as the "Restorer of Peace." He felt pangs of guilt when he recalled the days he called himself "the Master of All Things." The foolishness of youth!

Five years passed since that night. Again duty called. In spite of his faults, let no one ever say that Octavian shirked his duty. He was ill; he knew it. He knew he was dying. He welcomed death, longed for it. He wanted to see what lay beyond all human power and wisdom. He went to Brindisi to see Tiberias off on his eastern campaign. He would go as an emperor. He commanded the court to accompany him.

But this mightiest of the mighty never reached Brindisi. He fell sick. A mere cold, they said officially, a bout with influenza. But he knew it was old age; he was seventy-six years old. He could defeat Antony at Actium but he could not defeat death. His servants carried his frail body into the ancient, ancestral home of his father in Nola. He freed his faithful servants. Tiberias hurried from Brindisi to receive his final instructions. Octavian couldn't care less about the instructions. Well he knew Tiberias would do as he pleased. But for the good of the empire, he kept up appearances. Let them do as they please.

Livia, his faithful wife of fifty-two years, held him in her arms. The evening sun was setting behind the hills. He wished that he had visited this ancient home more often. He wished that Jesus of Nazareth was here. But the mighty emperor of the Romans could not even command that now. He knew he was dying.

He beckoned Livia to reach in his pocket. She dug out the small golden triangle. He feebly reached for it and held it as firmly as he could in his hand. He could not speak. His breathing became short and intermittent. He gasped for air. His arms fell to his side. The golden triangle fell from his hand to the marble floor. The sound of its falling shattered the silence of the room—and the world. The sound reverberated in a carpenter's shop in distant Galilee.

"Shalom!" said Jesus.